Essential
Jerusalem

by
GREER FAY CASHMAN

An Australian resident in Jerusalem, Greer Fay Cashman is a
journalist specialising in travel and tourism.

Little, Brown and Company
Boston Toronto London

FIRST U.S. EDITION

The contents of this publication are believed correct at the time of printing.
Nevertheless, the publishers cannot accept responsibility for errors or
omissions, nor for changes in details given. We are always grateful to
readers who let us know of any errors or omissions they come across, and
future printings will be updated accordingly.

Produced by the Publishing Division of The Automobile Association of
Great Britain.

Written by Greer Fay Cashman
"Peace and Quiet" section by Paul Sterry
Consultant: Frank Dawes

ISBN 0-316-25009-0

10 9 8 7 6 5 4 3 2 1

PRINTED IN TRENTO, ITALY

This book employs a
simple rating system to
help choose which
places to visit.

  do not miss

  see if you can

  worth seeing if
      you have time

INTRODUCTION

No one who visits Jerusalem remains indifferent to the charm of the city. The two most common expressions escaping the lips of first-time visitors are 'Isn't it beautiful!' and 'I never imagined it to be like this'.

One of the oldest cities in the world, it sits on the ridge of the Judean Mountains and overlooks the Judean Desert. In Biblical times the capital of the Kingdom of Israel, Jerusalem has been the capital, since 1948, of the sovereign State of Israel.

Widely proclaimed as the cradle of the three great faiths, Judaism, Christianity and Islam, Jerusalem is a showcase of ecumenism. Though the image of Jerusalem, as reflected by the international media, is one of a hotbed of political and religious controversy, very little of this is in evidence in the day-to-day comings and goings within the city. While differences between various ethnic and religious groups may occasionally erupt into sharp conflict, episodes of violence are short-lived, and in

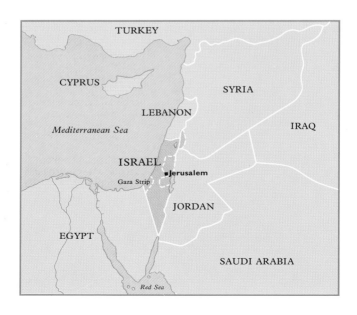

Jerusalem, the eternal city: a view over the ancient town and East Jerusalem to downtown West Jerusalem, the hub of the modern city. In the foreground is the Dome of the Rock

general, an atmosphere of harmony prevails. This spiritual co-existence is best experienced in the Old City, where the sounds of Jewish prayer at the Western ('Wailing') Wall are tempered by the echoes of church bells and the call of the muezzin.

The first-time visitor is often surprised to find so wide-ranging a mix of peoples within such a relatively small area: east and west, ancient and modern, religious and secular all meet in 42 square miles (108 sq km). The residents of Jerusalem come from well over a hundred ethnic and religious backgrounds. Many are first generation Israelis; some can trace their roots back 20 generations and more. Many inhabitants of the city, including young people, preserve the traditions of dress, cuisine, religious practice and customs handed down by their ancestors from one generation to another.

A ride on a city bus will give the visitor an idea of how these differences exist side by side: among the other passengers at any given time could be a cassocked priest from one of the Eastern churches, an Arab woman in a traditional long, black gown, the bodice of which is exquisitely hand-embroidered, an Ethiopian immigrant in flowing white robes, a black-garbed orthodox Jew with beard and cork-screw side curls, an Indian immigrant in a graceful sari, and a Yemenite whose colourful leggings extend beyond the hemline of her dress.

Some of the population are deeply devout; some are traditionalists; and others are completely secular. There are Christian Arabs and there are Muslim Arabs. There are Lutherans, Copts, Anglicans, Catholics belonging to a multitude of orders, members of the Greek Orthodox Church and Protestants of almost every persuasion. There are Ethiopians and there is a small Armenian community which preserves the language, customs and traditions of Armenia and lives in its own quarter. Jews, of course, far outnumber these, the main distinction among them being Sephardic Jews and Ashkenazic Jews.

Sephardic Jews are those whose ancestors lived in Spain or Portugal prior to the expulsion of Jews in 1492. They are distinguished from Ashkenazic Jews in that most of their cultural traditions and customs originated in Spain, whereas those of Ashkenazic Jews developed in northwest and central Europe, primarily in Germany, before making an impact in other countries. Jews lived in Germany in the 11th and 12th centuries, as evidenced from tombstone inscriptions in the ancient Jewish cemetery in Worms. It is possible that they may have settled there even earlier. Aside from Sephardic and Ashkenazic Jews, there are also those who settled in Muslim countries. Their customs and traditions are of course influenced by those practised in their host countries. The Yemenite Jews are believed to have more closely preserved the way of life of their forefathers who lived in ancient Israel. Similarly, there are Jews of French origin and there are Jews of Russian background who share some kind of national heritage with other representatives of their countries of origin.

Poverty and affluence constantly rub shoulders with each other. The distance between slums and wealthy neighbourhoods is negligible; sometimes, it is just a matter of crossing the road. The hub of the city, downtown West Jerusalem,

The Russian Orthodox Church of Mary Magdalene, on the Mount of Olives, is one of the most striking buildings in the city

is almost always congested, except for Saturdays when businesses are closed. The founding fathers of West Jerusalem, built up during only the last century, never envisaged that their sleepy little town would become a large, bustling motorised city. The streets are too narrow for the volume of traffic and it is not much better for pedestrians. Many of the older apartment blocks have no provision for car parking and in the absence of garages, car owners left their vehicles parked on the road. However, the density of traffic became so great that a few years ago a new ordinance was introduced which permitted parking on the sidewalk. Sometimes there are so many cars parked so close to each other that the unfortunate pedestrians have no alternative but to walk in the gutter.

In the Old City, in spite of the fact that it is well on the way to the 21st century in terms of electronic gadgets and sophisticated motorised transport, there are still those who ride on donkeys, camels and horses. The average Israeli family lives in a two-bedroom apartment.

INTRODUCTION

When there are a lot of children in the family, the living room is furnished with a sofa-bed which is used by the parents, who, for lack of financial resources, must sacrifice the privacy of their own bedroom in favour of their children.

There is little rented housing. Most people own their own apartments, which are progressively larger and less expensive the further away they are from the centre of town.

High-rise buildings are a comparatively recent phenomenon. When the Jerusalem Hilton hotel was constructed in the 1970s, there was a great deal of public controversy, because Jerusalemites were unused to skyscrapers. The hotel, standing out like a huge exclamation mark against the sky, is a sign to travellers coming up on the highway from Tel Aviv that they are approaching Jerusalem. Nowadays, despite continuing opposition from people who don't want anything to obstruct their view of heaven, more and more multi-storey residential and commercial towers are changing the look of the city skyline.

A feast for the eyes that can have changed little over the centuries

Jerusalem, the 'Eternal City', is above all a fascinating city of contrasts. Any visit is bound to be both moving and memorable.

BACKGROUND

One of the most ancient cities in the world, Jerusalem is first mentioned in the Egyptian Execration Texts of the 19th and 18th centuries before Christ. There is some evidence that humans lived in the area in the prehistoric period. Scholars believe that Man first inhabited what is today known as Jerusalem in the Pleistocene period. The city has survived numerous civilisations and conflagrations; it has been destroyed and rebuilt; it has been conquered and occupied by a series of foreign rulers. Since 1948, it has been the capital of the sovereign State of Israel, the seat of government and the domain of both the Supreme Court and the Chief Rabbinate. In the early 1950s it also became the city of residence of the President of the State.

Among the many charms of the city is the re-emergence of reminders of past civilisations. Archaeological teams have found the remains of houses, guard towers, places of worship and even a commercial centre which serve as wondrous bridges to the past.

In fact so many of these testaments to other eras have been unearthed in recent years that land development has become a gamble. Building contractors know that the chances are high that in digging the foundations for their new projects, they could bring to light long-hidden remnants from the Byzantine or even the Roman period.

When this happens, construction plans are laid aside, sometimes for indefinite periods, to enable large-scale excavation work. The most extensive and rewarding excavations have been carried out in and around the Old City. Visitors are permitted to join the digs and to share in the discoveries of coins minted more than a thousand years ago, a piece of Roman glass that was once part of a perfume bottle or an everyday utensil which may well have served the needs of some noble family in the period prior to the destruction, in AD70, of the Second Temple.

But it is not a case of finders, keepers. These antique treasures belong to the State of Israel and must be given by those who discover them into the custody of the representatives of the Antiquities Authority who are supervising the dig.

The Jerusalem Foundation, which initiates new projects, oversees the maintenance of existing projects and promotes Jerusalem at home and abroad, is gearing up for the celebrations in 1996 of the 3,000th anniversary of the city. A think-tank of public relations and communications experts has been appointed to formulate a year-long programme of events relating to Jerusalem throughout the ages. One possibility is a Davidic convention aimed at bringing together as many people as possible bearing the name of Israel's second king, whose first claim to fame was the slaying of the great Philistine warrior Goliath with so simple a weapon as a sling-shot.

BACKGROUND

Jerusalem of the Bible

Jerusalem was mentioned in the Old Testament long before the advent of David—the first reference is in the 14th chapter of the *Book of Genesis*—but few chroniclers concern themselves greatly with the history of the city prior to its conquest by David. In taking it from the Jebusites, he elevated its importance, and soon after made it the capital of the country. At that time, approximately 1,000BC, Jerusalem had neither geographic nor economic advantages. It was only after King Solomon came to the throne in 965BC that Jerusalem began to develop as an economic centre. It became the crossroads for caravans travelling from the Euphrates to Egypt and from Phoenicia to the Red Sea. Though David had talked of building a holy Temple, the actual task of doing so fell to Solomon. Thus the construction of the First Temple and the adjacent royal palace gave Jerusalem both a spiritual and a regal character. Following Solomon's death in 926BC, there was a split in the monarchy. Jerusalem remained the capital of the small Kingdom of Judah and the seat of the Davidic dynasty.

In the ensuing years, Jerusalem became a religious battleground in which paganism often triumphed. In 587BC, the city was conquered and plundered by King Nebuchadnezzar of Babylon, who destroyed the First Temple. A large percentage of the population was sent into exile and the ruined city declined.

The Persian and Hellenistic Period

In 539BC, Babylon was conquered by Persia's Cyrus the Great, who restored to the exiled Jerusalemites the holy vessels which Nebuchadnezzar had taken from the Temple. Seeking allies among the exiles, he also permitted them to return to Jerusalem. Resettlement was gradual, but one of their first projects was the rebuilding of the Temple. The Second Temple was completed in 515BC, but the city was still grossly underpopulated. It was not until 445BC that any serious effort was made to restore the city to its former glory.

The Persian period was followed by the Hellenistic period, the start of which was marked by the peaceful conquest in 332BC of the Kingdom of Judah and, with it, Jerusalem. Under Alexander the Great, Jerusalem continued to prosper, but after his death in 323BC, the city again began to deteriorate. Jerusalem was attacked by Ptolemy I, the King of Egypt, who, legend has it, won the battle with ease because the inhabitants of the city refused to fight on the Sabbath.

In 198BC, the city was seized by the Seleucids who granted the Jews a charter whereby they were permitted to live in accordance with the laws of their forefathers. The charter, however, was a sham. Matters came to a head in 167BC when the Temple was desecrated by Antiochus Epiphanes, who had ascended the throne in 175BC. The violation sparked the Hasmonean revolt led by Judah Macabeus, which resulted in the

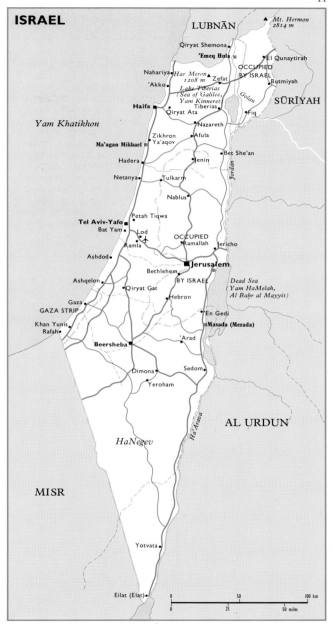

ISRAEL

LUBNĀN

▲ Mt. Hermon
2814 m

Qiryat Shemona

'Emeq Hula
• El Qunaytirah

OCCUPIED
BY ISRAEL

Nahariya
'Akko
Har Meron
1208 m
Zefat
Butmiyah

Haifa
Qiryat Ata
Lake Tiberias
(Sea of Galilee,
Yam Kinneret)
Tiberias

Golan

SŪRĪYAH

Fiq

Yam Khatikhon

Nazareth

Zikhron
Ya'aqov
Afula

Ma'agan Mikhael

Bet She'an

Hadera
Jenin

Netanya
Tulkarm

Nablus

Petah Tiqwa

Tel Aviv-Yafo
Bat Yam
Lod
Ramla

Jordan

OCCUPIED
Ramallah
Jericho

Ashdod

Bethlehem
Jerusalem

Ashqelon
BY ISRAEL

Dead Sea
(Yam HaMelah,
Al Bahr al Mayyit)

Qiryat Gat

Gaza
Hebron

GAZA STRIP
En Gedi

Khan Yunis
Masada (Mezada)
Rafah

Beersheba

'Arad

Sedom

Dimona

Yeroham

AL URDUN

HaNegev

Ha'Arava

MISR

Yotvata

Eilat (Elat)

| 0 | | 50 | | 100 km |
| 0 | 25 | | 50 miles | |

purging of the Temple from all things pagan. Jerusalem remained under Hasmonean rule for a century, during which time it became strong and prosperous, albeit not always peaceful. In 63BC, the two sons of Salome, Hyrcanus and Aristobulus, fighting with each other over who was to succeed their mother, turned to Rome for help. Pompey, the Roman general, chose Hyrcanus, leaving the administration of the city to him and to his adviser Antipater, whose son Herod became king in 37BC and continued to reign for 33 years. A much-hated man, Herod was a great builder, and while in power, greatly enhanced the beauty of the city. Remains of some of the Herodian edifices can still be seen in Jerusalem.

Roman and Byzantine Rule

After Herod's son Archelaus was deposed as governor in AD7, Judea was merged in the Roman province of Syria. Among the procurators of Jerusalem was Pontius Pilate, who constructed the first aqueduct enabling the transfer of water from the Hebron region to Jerusalem. Pontius Pilate is less remembered for this gift of life than for his execution of Christ. Resistance to Roman rule was only a matter of time. The first stirrings of an uprising began in AD66, culminating four years later in a full-scale war and the burning of the city by Titus, son of the Emperor Vespasian. The Temple was engulfed in flame. Those residents of the city who did not die in battle later perished from hunger. The city

remained in ruins for 61 years. In 130 the Roman Emperor Hadrian, during a visit to Jerusalem, decided to build a Roman colony over the ruins of the Jewish city. In accordance with Roman custom, he ordered the ploughing and furrowing of the area where the walls of the colony were to be constructed. It was this act which sparked the Bar Kokhba revolt. The victorious Jews forced the Romans to evacuate the city which, for three years, again became Jewish, and a provisional Temple was built. The Romans again conquered the city in the third summer of the Bar Kokhba revolt, when Hadrian banned all circumcised males from the city. The superior Roman building techniques from this period have survived the test of time, as today's visitors to the Old City can testify.

The Roman period was followed by the Byzantine era. Although many of the anti-Jewish laws had been repealed during the reign of Emperor Antonius Pius, who ruled from 138 to 161, it was Constantine the Great who, in 313, introduced the edict of tolerance which gave full religious freedom to the residents of Aelia Capitolina, which was the name which Hadrian had given to Jerusalem. In 326, what Christians believe to be the True Cross was discovered in a crypt beneath the ruined Temple of Venus. This discovery marked the area of Christ's burial site. At the urging of his mother, Constantine decided to do due honour to the hallowed place by erecting the Church of the Holy Sepulchre over Christ's tomb. Another important church, the Eleona, was built on the Mount of Olives. These two structures gave Jerusalem a pre-eminently Christian character and the city developed as a major Christian centre. Jews were again expelled and permitted to enter only once a year on the anniversary of the destruction of the Temple.

When Julian the Apostate became emperor in 361, he permitted Jews to return to Jerusalem and to begin rebuilding the Temple. From then until the 7th century, Jews were intermittently banished from the city.

Islam

The Muslim conquest of Jerusalem took place in 638 in a bloodless coup led by Caliph Omar. The original site of the Temple had been reduced to a garbage dump. Omar had it cleaned and laid the foundations for the El Aqsa mosque. Seventy Jewish families were allowed to take up residence, but though many Arabs subsequently settled in Jerusalem, the city remained predominantly Christian.

In 878, Jerusalem, along with the rest of Palestine, was annexed to the Egyptian kingdom of Ahmad ibn Tulun. If there had been intolerance among the various religious groups before, there was now outright hatred; yet, despite the hostilities between Christians, Jews and Muslims, each of the religious movements developed and gained new followers. But animosities festered and in 1009, the Fatimid

The layout of the Old City's four quarters (above, the Muslim sector) dates back to Roman-Byzantine times

Caliph al-Hakim ordered the destruction of all Christian buildings other than the Church of the Nativity in Bethlehem. This action shocked the Christian world, but response was slow. In 1071, Jerusalem was conquered by the Seljuks, who annexed the city to the Turkish Empire, and fighting continued until the arrival of the Crusaders.

BACKGROUND

The Crusaders

The Crusaders' siege of Jerusalem began on 6 June 1099 and lasted until 15 July, when they took the city and massacred the bulk of the population. In the second century of their rule, the Crusaders sought to repopulate the city and brought in Christian Arabs from Transjordan whom they settled in the sector between the Damascus and Lions' Gates. The status of Jerusalem was enhanced as the capital of the Crusader kingdom and in the course of time this had a favourable effect on the economy. The 12th century witnessed a frenzy of building and the establishment of many Christian traditions.

The Crusaders were defeated in 1187. Jerusalem surrendered to Salah-a-Din and many of the holy Christian places became Muslim shrines and schools. Salah-a-Din encouraged the return of Jews to Jerusalem.

The Damascus Gate, a fine example of Ottoman defensive architecture

Mamluks and Ottomans

From 1260 until the Ottoman conquest of 1516/17, all of Palestine was under the rule of the Mamluks, who had conquered Syria, Egypt and the Mongols. Jerusalem, during this period, was a theological capital, but its economy disintegrated. The overwhelming majority of the residents were Muslims; there were some 1,000 Christians and a slightly smaller number of Jews. Muslim theologians wielded considerable influence and were largely responsible for persecution against minority groups in the population. If the Muslims made life miserable for the Christians, the Christians in turn made life intolerable for the Jews. The Mamluks were also harsh towards the Jews and in 1440 imposed such heavy taxes on the Jews of Jerusalem that those who could not afford to pay them had no choice other than to leave the city. However, there was never a period in which Jerusalem was totally bereft of Jews.

The first Ottoman king of Jerusalem was Selim I, but it was Suleiman the Magnificent who left the most lasting imprint on the city. It was he who built the present wall surrounding the Old City, on top of ruins, some of which dated to the period of the Second Temple. Suleiman also ensured the improvement of Jerusalem's water supply. He was sympathetic to the Jews and allowed them to restore Jewish cultural and religious life in Jerusalem.

Jerusalem remained under Ottoman rule until 1917. European powers evinced growing interest in the city during the 18th century and in the 19th century began opening consulates. There was also heightened Christian activity. The first Christian settlements outside the walls of the Old City were inaugurated in the 1850s. The breathtaking Notre Dame Hospice opposite the New Gate is one of the more spectacular buildings outside the walls. Other Christian projects outside the walls of the Old City include the American Colony, construction of which commenced in 1881, the Sisters of the Rosary Convent in 1884, the St Vincent de Paul Hospice (1888), the St Louis Hospital (1889), and the Leper Hospital (1887). Jewish settlement outside the walls took a little longer, and were it not for an epidemic which drove residents of the Old City to seek a healthier environment, it might never have taken place at all. It started off with the founding in 1860 of Mishkenot Sha'ananim, and was followed in the 1880s with Ohel Moshe, Mazkeret Moshe, Batei Ungarim (in Me'a She'arim), the Diskin Orphanage, Mahane Yehuda and Sha'arei Zedek.

The Twentieth Century

In 1917, the Ottoman rule of Jerusalem came to an end. The British forces under the command of General Allenby entered the city in December of that year, and the territory remained under British military administration until July 1920. It was then replaced by a civil administration. The Balfour Declaration of November 1917 had virtually guaranteed the future establishment of a sovereign Jewish State. What it failed to do was to determine exactly when this would come about: some of the British soldiers stationed in Palestine gave the impression that Israel's independence would never come to fruition.

Under the British administration, the municipal council functioned as an ecumenical body. Initially it comprised two Jews, two Christians and two Muslims. Later there were three representatives of each community and in 1924 the number was increased to four. This balance could not be maintained in the face of the city's development. In 1934, the city was divided into 12 constituencies, each of which elected its own representative to sit on the council.

Muslim riots, with occasional Jewish reprisals, broke out in 1929 and again in 1936. In 1937 Jewish retaliation intensified. This in turn resulted in greater militancy on the part of the Arabs, which again drew more concentrated reprisals from the Jews. Some of the Jewish residents joined the British Army, but others, angered by the anti-Zionist policy adopted by Britain in 1939, became involved in anti-British sabotage operations. The Arabs also mounted attacks against the British. Jewish outrage against the British knew no bounds in the aftermath of World War II when British forces turned back refugees who had survived the Nazi holocaust.

November 1947 was a milestone in Jewish aspirations for nationhood. It was then that the United Nations voted for the partition of Palestine. This was also the signal for a new wave of hostilities between Jews and Arabs. In May 1948, only 12 days after the declaration of the sovereign State of Israel, the Jewish Quarter of the Old City surrendered to the Jordanian army. The younger men who had participated in the fighting were taken prisoner. The elderly men, together with women and children—some 1,300 people all told—were evacuated to the New City. A general cease-fire was declared in June 1948. East Jerusalem remained in Transjordanian hands and West Jerusalem in Israeli hands. The size of the population at that time was slightly more than one fifth of what it is today.

For 19 years, Jerusalem remained a divided city. On 5 June 1967, Jordanian forces seized the UN headquarters, thus triggering the Six Days War which culminated in the Israeli occupation of the West Bank. Restoration work began on Jewish properties which had been damaged in the interim. Archaeological research was resumed. There was an immigration boom, which under the rules of supply and demand generated a housing boom. Understandably, the Arabs in East Jerusalem were not exactly overjoyed at the advent of an Israeli administration. There were job openings in West Jerusalem; and the general influx of tourism brought smiles to the faces of the merchants.

The smiles began to fade in December 1987 with the outbreak of the *intifada*. Frustrated by 20 years of Israeli occupation, the Palestinians decided to speed up the process of acquiring their own homeland by making life tough for the Jews. Occasionally non-Jews and non-Muslims get caught in the crossfire. In addition to loss of life, the *intifada* has caused loss of income in both East and West Jerusalem. A fall-off in tourists has affected hotels in both sections of the city. Moreover, East Jerusalem merchants have their shops open only for very brief periods each day. The colourful character of the Arab bazaar has been dulled to a pale shadow of what it used to be. The situation is likely to remain unsettled until such time as there is an acceptable resolution to Palestinian aspirations.

WHAT TO SEE

East Jerusalem—The Old City

For the historian, the sociologist and the tourist, the most fascinating sector of Jerusalem is undoubtedly that part of the city walled in by ancient stone. For it is in the Old City that one can truly come into contact with past civilisations and almost literally walk in the footsteps of Jesus. It is here that so many aspects of scripture cease to be a mere Bible lesson and take on elements of reality. It is here that one finds the greatest concentration of all the weaves incorporated in Israel's social fabric.

The maze of winding streets can sometimes be confusing and if you're in a hurry, you would do well to pay a young boy a modest sum—preferably in

Ancient history and modern life go hand in hand within the walls of the Old City

dollars or sterling—to lead you to the Western Wall, the Temple Mount, the Church of the Holy Sepulchre or one of the gates in the wall surrounding the Old City. Most of the shopkeepers speak fairly good English, and all have young helpers whom they can despatch to show you the way if you should happen to lose your bearings.

Museums of interest are listed separately on pages 60–67.

◆

ALEXANDRA HOSPICE

opposite the Church of the Redeemer

Primarily of interest to visitors of Russian background, the Alexandra Hospice incorporates the Russian Orthodox Church, which was built in the 19th century. The site contains architectural remains dating back to the time of Hadrian and of Herod.

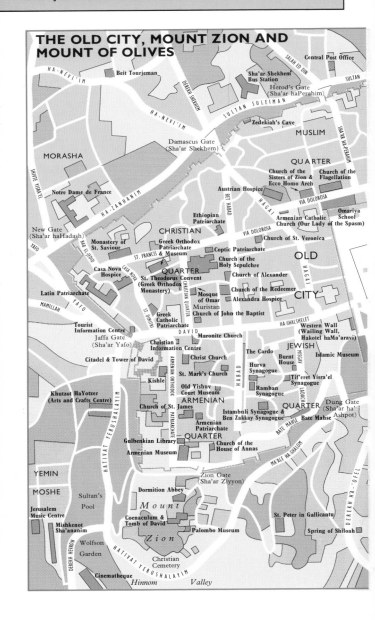

THE OLD CITY, MOUNT ZION AND MOUNT OF OLIVES

SALAH ED DIN

Central Post Office

HA-NEVI'IM

Beit Tourjeman

DEREKH SHEKHEM

Sha'ar Shekhem Bus Station

Herod's Gate (Sha'ar haPerahim)

SULTAN

SULTAN SULEIMAN

SHA'AR HA-PERAHIM

HA-NEVI'IM

Zedekiah's Cave

MUSLIM

Damascus Gate (Sha'ar Shekhem)

MORASHA

SHIVTE YISRA'EL

HA-ZANHANIM

Notre Dame de France

New Gate (Sha'ar haHadash)

YAFO

BAR EL-EDDID

CASA NOVA

Monastery of St. Saviour

ST. FRANCIS & MUSEUM

Casa Nova Hospice

Latin Patriarchate

MAMILLAH

YAFO

ST. DIMITRI

Austrian Hospice

BET HABAD

QUARTER

Church of the Sisters of Zion & Ecco Homo Arch

Church of the Flagellation

HAGAI

VIA DOLOROSA

Armenian Catholic Church (Our Lady of the Spasm)

Omariya School

Ethiopian Patriarchate

CHRISTIAN

Greek Orthodox Patriarchate & Museum

Coptic Patriarchate

Church of the Holy Sepulchre

QUARTER

St. Theodorus Convent (Greek Orthodox Monastery)

Mosque of Omar

Muristan

Church of John the Baptist

Greek Catholic Patriarchate

Church of Alexander

VIA DOLOROSA

Church of St. Veronica

OLD

Church of the Redeemer

Alexandra Hospice

HAGAI

CITY

HA-SHALSHELET

Western Wall (Wailing Wall, Hakotel haMa'aravi)

Tourist Information Centre

Jaffa Gate (Sha'ar Yafo)

Citadel & Tower of David

DAVID

Maronite Church

Christian Information Centre

Christ Church

ARMENIAN ORTHODOX

Kishle

St. Mark's Church

The Cardo

JEWISH

Burnt House

MISGAV

Islamic Museum

HABAD

Hurva Synagogue

Khutzot HaYotzer (Arts and Crafts Centre)

HATIVAT YERUSHALAYIM

Old Yishuv Court Museum

Church of St. James

ARMENIAN

Ramban Synagogue

Tif'eret Yisra'el Synagogue

LADACH

Istambuli Synagogue & Ben Zakkay Synagogue

QUARTER

Dung Gate (Sha'ar ha' Ashpot)

Armenian Patriarchate

PATRIARCHATE

QUARTER

BATE MAHSE

Bate Mahse

Gulbenkian Library

Armenian Museum

Church of the House of Annas

MA'ALE HASHALOM

DEREKH HA-OFEL

YEMIN

MOSHE

Jerusalem Music Centre

Mishkenot Sha'ananim

DEREKH HEVRON

Wolfson Garden

Sultan's Pool

Zion Gate (Sha'ar Ziyyon)

Dormition Abbey

Mount

Coenaculum & Tomb of David

Zion

HATIVAT YERUSHALAYIM

Christian Cemetery

Palombo Museum

St. Peter in Gallicantu

Spring of Shiloah

Cinematheque

Hinnom   *Valley*

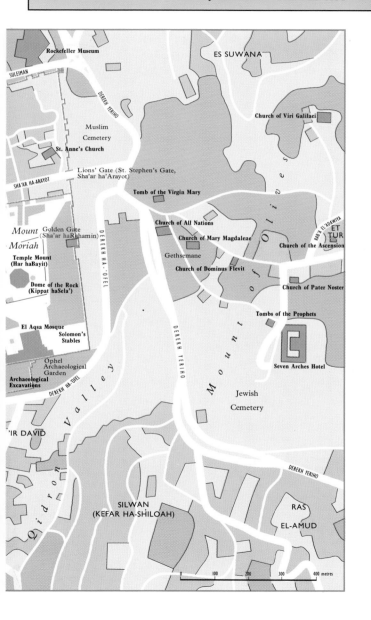

Rockefeller Museum

ES SUWANA

SULEIMAN

DEREKH YERIHO

Muslim Cemetery

Church of Viri Galilaei

St. Anne's Church

SHA'AR HA-ARAYOT

Lions' Gate (St. Stephen's Gate, Sha'ar ha'Arayot)

Tomb of the Virgin Mary

Mount Moriah

Golden Gate (Sha'ar haRhamin)

Temple Mount (Har haBayit)

DEREKH HA-'OFEL

Church of All Nations

Church of Mary Magdaleae

Gethsemane

Church of Dominus Flevit

AB'A EL-ADAWIYA

ET TUR

Church of the Ascension

Church of Pater Noster

Dome of the Rock (Kippat haSela')

El Aqsa Mosque

Solomon's Stables

Tombs of the Prophets

Ophel Archaeological Garden

DEREKH YERIHO

Mount of Olives

Archaeological Excavations

DEREKH HA-'OFEL

Seven Arches Hotel

'IR DAVID

Qidron Valley

Jewish Cemetery

DEREKH YERIHO

SILWAN (KEFAR HA-SHILOAH)

RAS EL-AMUD

0   100   200   300   400 metres

ARMENIAN QUARTER
southwest Old City

The small, but fiercely proud Armenian community lives mainly in the southwest of the Old City. The Armenian Church of St James is part of a monastery dating back to the 7th century. It is the focal point of the walled-in Armenian compound, which is accessible from the Jaffa Gate on the one side and the Zion Gate on the other (these gates close early each evening). The Armenian Quarter contains a library, printing press, museum, school and cemetery. The continued existence of the Armenian community as a minority group, heavily outnumbered by Christians of other persuasions, Muslims and Jews, is a remarkable phenomenon. The significance of the Jerusalem Armenian Patriarchate can be traced back to its early beginnings in the 12th century, at which time there were numerous Armenian monasteries in the Holy Land. During the Mamluk and Ottoman periods the Armenian Patriarchate was the leader of all the Christian communities here. The **Church of St James**, built over the ruins of an ancient Byzantine church, was constructed in the 11th century. The house of worship commemorates both James, the brother of Jesus, and James the Apostle, the brother of John the Evangelist, who in AD44 was beheaded by Herod Agrippa. *Open:* Monday to Friday 3:00/ 3:30 P.M.; Saturday, Sunday 2:30/ 5:15 P.M.

The Armenians played a major role in the development of Jerusalem, setting up the city's first printing press, the **St James Printing Press**, which, together with the **Gulbenkian Library**, is located just south of the Church of St James.
Open: Monday to Saturday 10:00 A.M.–5:00 P.M.

Also located within the compound is the **Church of the House of Annas** (sometimes known as the Convent of the Olive Tree). The 14th-century building was constructed on the site believed to have been that of the house of Annas, the father-in-law of Caiaphas, the High Priest to whom Jesus was brought by the Romans. An olive tree in the courtyard is said to be a descendant of that to which Jesus was bound during the period of his imprisonment. *Open:* Saturday 3:00/4:00 P.M.

The Armenian Museum contains many artefacts from previous civilisations. See page 60.
Buses: 3, 13, 19, 20 serve the Armenian Quarter

◆
CHRIST CHURCH
inside the Jaffa Gate

Opposite the rear gate of the Citadel is Christ Church, the first Anglican church in the Ottoman Empire. The site on which it stands was purchased in 1838 by the London Society for Promoting Christianity Amongst the Jews. The site was consecrated in January 1849, though construction commenced in 1841. Gothic in style, the building is surrounded by a pleasant courtyard. Adjacent to the church is an Anglican hospice for pilgrims.

The Greek Orthodox community is one of many represented in the churches of the Christian quarter

◆◆◆
CHRISTIAN QUARTER
northwest Old City
This is indeed pilgrims' paradise, including as it does numerous religious sites and churches. The Christian Quarter is distinguished by the **Church of the Holy Sepulchre**, (see page 22). Other sites and institutions of note include the **Monastery of St Saviour**, belonging to the Franciscan Order and dating back to the beginning of the 17th century; the **Latin Patriarchate**, which is the seat of the Roman Catholic Church in Israel, Jordan and Cyprus, and which was established in 1099; the **Casa Nova Hospice** established by the Franciscans in 1866; **St**

Theodorus Convent, a 6th-century Greek Orthodox monastery; the **Greek Catholic Patriarchate**; the **Greek Orthodox Museum** (see under **Museums**) housed in the **Greek Orthodox Patriarchate**; the **Ethiopian Patriarchate; the Coptic Patriarchate; the Church of the Redeemer** (see page 23); the **Church of John the Baptist**, restored by the Greek Orthodox community in 1842 on the ruins of a Crusader church; **Coptic Khan**, a pilgrims' hostel run by the Copts since 1838; and many schools and libraries. The interior opulence of most of these properties is often quite a revelation following the plainness of the façades.
Muristan, sitting to the north of David Street, was once occupied by the Forum of Aelia Capitolina. In the 5th century the site was chosen by Queen Eudoxia for the construction of a hospital for the residents of Jerusalem (the Persian word for hospital is *muristan*). This was subsequently destroyed by the Muslims and in its place a hospice was constructed for pilgrims coming from the west. In time, a library, a monastery and the Church of Santa Maria Latina were added. The monastery was dedicated to St John. In Crusader times, its warden gave shelter to several Crusader knights who had been wounded in the siege of Jerusalem. Those who recovered were subsequently known as the Knights of St John of the Hospital, forerunners of the Knights of Malta.
Buses: 3, 13, 19, 20 serve the Christian Quarter

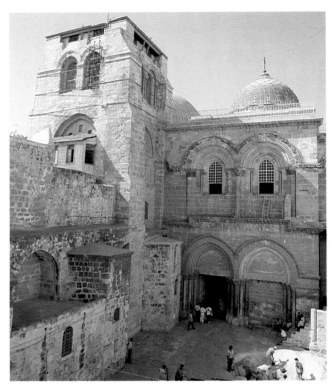

◆◆◆
CHURCH OF THE HOLY SEPULCHRE

The Church of the Holy Sepulchre, the holiest site in Christendom

centre of Old City
All streets in the Old City eventually lead to the Church of the Holy Sepulchre, though pilgrims usually go from St Stephen's Gate, which in Hebrew is known as Lions' Gate. No other shrine in Christendom can rival this one, for this is the site of the crucifixion and burial of Christ. In the very heart of the Christian Quarter, the Church of the Holy Sepulchre has, like so many other structures in the city, fallen victim to ravages wrought both by nature and by conquering armies. The present Church is the fourth to be constructed on the site since the Emperor Constantine's original 4th-century church. Totally destroyed during the Persian invasion of Jerusalem in 614, it was rebuilt by Theodosius, destroyed again by Caliph Hakim in 1009, and partially

restored 40 years later. The present-day Crusader church was built in 1149, but has undergone many changes as a result of fires and earthquakes. In the late 1950s, major restoration work was carried out by the Greek, Armenian and Latin churches.

Although one would expect the Church of the Holy Sepulchre to be a symbol of peace and harmony, the opposite is true. Since the 11th century it has been the subject of ongoing squabbles among various sectors of the Christian community. Hostilities grew as the different groups vied for ownership. In the final analysis, each denomination constructed a chapel of its own. The communities responsible for the Church today are the Roman Catholic, Greek Orthodox, Armenian, Syrian, Coptic and Abyssinian, with the lion's share held by the Greek Orthodox. Five of the Stations of the Cross are contained within the Church of the Holy Sepulchre, whose crypts, tombs, chapels and cloisters rival each other in beauty, and often in sound. Each of the warring factions delights in creating various distractions while one of the other factions is at prayer.

The visitor's eye falls first on the Stone of Unction, a red slab of limestone placed over the spot where the body of Christ was removed from the Cross and anointed prior to entombment. The Stone of Unction is jointly owned by all six denominations represented in the Church, but another nearby stone slab, known as the Place of the Three Marys, belongs to the Armenians. The rotunda is the only part of the Church which still bears any resemblance to Constantine's Church of the Resurrection. The Holy Sepulchre is in the very centre of the rotunda. To gain a proper appreciation of all the chapels, crypts and tombs, the visitor needs to spend at least three hours wandering from one to another. A great deal of the city's history is encapsulated in this area. The most important of the chapels is Golgatha or Calvary, where Christ was stripped and crucified. Also of interest is the altar of Mary Magdalene, constructed by the Roman Catholics to commemorate the place where the resurrected Christ appeared to Mary Magdalene; and the Chapel of Adam, where Adam's skull was said to be buried.

Open: 4:30 A.M.–8:00 P.M.; winter until 7:00 P.M.
Buses: 1, 3, 13, 19, 20, 23, 38

◆◆
CHURCH OF THE REDEEMER
centre of Old City
During his visit to the Holy Land in 1869, Crown Prince Friedrich Wilhelm of Prussia purchased a parcel of land in the Muristan district of the Christian Quarter. The area, which had been in ruins for centuries, was designated as the site for the German Evangelical Lutheran Church of the Redeemer. The building was consecrated on the last day of the year 1898. The premises are often used for recitals of classical music. The belfry offers one of the best aerial views of the Old City.

CITADEL AND TOWER OF DAVID
Jaffa Gate

The tower of David is one of three erected by Herod the Great, and was originally named the Tower of Phasael in honour of Herod's brother. When Titus destroyed Jerusalem in AD70 he left the towers as silent, stone witnesses to the Roman conquest. The Citadel, which today houses a museum telling the story of Jerusalem throughout the ages, has always been a strategic point in the city's defences.

The Tower of David is nowadays the focal point of an absorbing Sound and Light show (see **Museums**, section under **Tower of David**).

CITY OF DAVID AND WARREN'S SHAFT
Temple Mount

The heart of Jerusalem at the time of the First Temple was the City of David and the Temple Mount (see separate entry, page 32). However, the ravages of time have left little of special interest apart from the underground water system, known today as Warren's Shaft. This installation gave the Israelites access to the waters of the Gihon Spring outside the city walls. From the City of David a sloping tunnel led to a vertical shaft plunging to the level of the Gihon Spring. This shaft can be visited today via a spiral staircase. An illuminated model explains the structure and function of the shaft.

Open: Sunday to Thursday, 9:00 A.M.–5:00 P.M.; Friday until 1:00 P.M.

Buses: 1, 3

COENACULUM
Mount Zion

Reputed to be the chamber in which Christ ate his Last Supper in the company of his disciples, this room is located on the upper floor of the building on Mount Zion whose lower floor is said to contain the tomb of King David. The room has great meaning only to the devout. Anyone entering and not knowing its history would be unlikely to feel any divine presence.

DAMASCUS GATE
north Old City

Guests at the Pilgrims Palace Hotel like to look out of the window of the upstairs lounge, which offers a perfect view of the comings and goings at the Damascus Gate across the road. Always impressive, it was built in the 16th century by Suleiman the Magnificent and is flanked by two towers and is accessible from the highway outside the Old City walls via a small amphitheatre where street vendors often gather to hawk their wares. Excavations beneath the gate have unearthed exciting finds which date from Roman and Crusader periods.

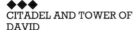

DOME OF THE ROCK
Temple Mount

Among the most revered of Muslim monuments in the city, the Dome of the Rock, an ornate

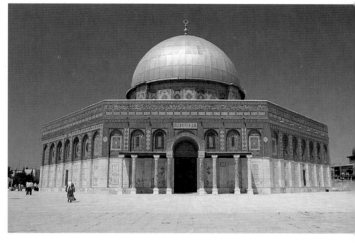

The Dome of the Rock: its walls are decorated with exquisite blue tiling

example of the best in Middle Eastern architecture, was erected in AD691 by Caliph Abd al-Malik, who was the ninth successor of the Prophet Mohammed. The magnificent edifice is one of the most outstanding landmarks of Jerusalem. It has been renovated many times by a succession of Muslim leaders, though Suleiman the Magnificent can claim credit for the unique mosaics which emphasise the Eastern characteristics of the structure. Built on the very site where the ancient Jewish High Priest entered the Holy of Holies sanctuary, the octagonal building, or more accurately the area where it is, has been a source of never-ending conflict between Muslims and Jews.
Open: daily except Fridays and Muslim holidays
Buses: 1, 38

DORMITION ABBEY
Mount Zion
Gracing the top of Mount Zion, this exquisitely beautiful church is an eternal memorial to Mary, mother of Christ. According to Christian legend, it was at this place that she entered the sleep from which there is no waking (hence 'dormition'). The land on which the church was built was presented by Sultan Abdul-Hamid to Kaiser Wilhelm II during the latter's visit to Jerusalem in 1898. Construction of the Church by German Catholics began in 1906 and the building was completed in 1910. Like so many other grand churches, the Dormition Abbey is a concert hall for classical music in addition to being a house of worship.
Open: 7:00 A.M.–12:30 P.M., 2:00 P.M.–7:10 P.M.

◆
DUNG GATE
south Old City
Of all the gates providing entry into the Old City, the Dung Gate is the closest of all to the Western Wall. The Dung Gate is mentioned in the Bible in the *Book of Nehemiah*. As its name indicates, it is the gate through which the refuse of the city was transported and cast into the Qidron Valley. Because of its proximity to the village of Silwan, it is sometimes called the Silwan Gate. In Crusader times, it was called the Gate of the Tanners.

◆◆◆
EL AQSA MOSQUE
Temple Mount
The main centre of Islamic religious activity in Israel, the El Aqsa Mosque dates back to the 8th century. In the early part of the 12th century, the Crusaders used it as a palace, but it resumed its Islamic identity in 1187 when Saladin recaptured Jerusalem. The scene of many dramas over the centuries, the mosque was defiled in July 1951 by the murder of Jordanian ruler King Abdallah who had come to pray. In 1969, an Australian tourist set fire to the mosque. Since then it has been the scene of many violent conflicts erupting in stone throwing and gun shots.
Open: daily except Fridays and Muslim holidays
Buses: 1, 38

◆
HEROD'S GATE
north Old City
One of the many impressive entry-ways into the Old City, this gate received its name in error:

Herod's Gate, an impressive entry-way, leads into the Muslim quarter of the Old City

15th-century researchers mistakenly believed that Herod's palace had been located in the immediate vicinity. In Hebrew, the gate is called *Sha'ar HaPerahim* and in Arabic, *Bab el-Zahira*. Both mean 'Gate of Flowers'.

◆◆
HURVA SYNAGOGUE
Jewish Quarter
In the midst of the Jewish Quarter is a huge, reconstructed arch which is virtually all that is left of the once majestic Hurva Synagogue. Construction of the building began in 1699 when Rabbi Yehuda the Hassid came to Jerusalem from Poland with 500 of his followers. His disciples took loans for the financing of the project from the wealthy Muslims of Jerusalem. Unfortunately, they could not find

the means of repaying these loans, as a result of which their angry creditors burnt the building to the ground. The ruins (*Hurva* means 'ruins') remained untouched for 150 years, but in the middle of the 19th century Baron Alphonse de Rothschild and Sir Moses Montefiore undertook to finance the rebuilding of the synagogue, which was opened with due pomp and ceremony in 1864. Bathed in natural light and one of the grandest structures in the city, the Hurva quickly became the pivotal point of Jewish life. During the War of Independence, it was one of the Israeli forces' strategic posts. The battle was won by the Jordanians, who destroyed the synagogue. After the Six Days War, the courtyard and the arch were restored, but plans to rebuild the synagogue were shelved.

◆
ISTAMBULI SYNAGOGUE
Jewish Quarter
The last of four Sephardic (see Introduction, page 6) synagogues constructed in the Jewish Quarter during the Ottoman period, the Istambuli Synagogue was financed by immigrants from Istanbul. It was built in 1764 and renovated in 1835. At the time of its renovation it was refurbished with an exquisitely carved and gilded ark which had been brought from Italy. Although there are other impressively designed synagogues, what makes this one especially important is that it stands over a large water cistern. According to Jewish

tradition, the sins of the old year must be cast into the sea or the river on the Jewish New Year, known in Hebrew as *Rosh Hashana*. Where there is no sea or river, the special prayer service of *Tashlich* is held at the opening of a well or cistern.

◆◆◆
JAFFA GATE
west Old City
One of the most important and best-known gates in the wall surrounding the Old City, the Jaffa Gate serves as a direct link between the Old City and the New City. The stream of human, four-legged and motorised traffic passing in both directions through the Jaffa Gate is probably greater in volume than through all the other gates put together. A tourist information office is just inside the gate, and a short distance away is the Christian Information Office.

◆◆◆
JEWISH QUARTER
southeast Old City
Not surprisingly, Jews began flocking back to the Jewish Quarter almost immediately after the Israeli victory in the Six Days War of June 1967. The rubble of war and neglect was cleared away over a period of time; old buildings were restored; new buildings were constructed; historical finds were unearthed in ongoing excavation projects. One of these is the **Cardo**, otherwise known as the Street of the Pillars. Running north to south, it was a major road in Roman and Byzantine Jerusalem. The Company for the Development of the Jewish

A stone arch sweeps over the ruins of the Hurva (meaning 'ruin') synagogue in the Jewish quarter

Quarter has built a modern commercial centre around the ancient Roman columns. At the end of the commercial centre is a turn-off leading to the Arab bazaar and the Damascus Gate. Characterised by winding lanes and public squares, the Jewish Quarter in its hey-day contained no less than 58 synagogues as well as numerous religious seminaries, better known as *yeshivot*. This concentration of houses of worship and houses of study brought many famous scholars to the city and

necessitated the construction of special residential quarters. Among the best-known of these is **Bate Mahse**, construction of which took place in the second half of the 19th century. It was a scene of bitter fighting during the War of Independence. Just as there are many artists in the Yemin Moshe neighbourhood beyond the walls, a high ratio of creative people have chosen to make their homes in the Jewish Quarter inside the walls. In the summer months they attract many visitors to arts and crafts fairs which are held outdoors in the main square. Another significant feature of the Jewish Quarter is the extraordinary number of museums, in particular the **Old Yishuv Court Museum** (see under **Museums**), which gives a good picture of life here in the 19th century.

◆
KISHLE
south of Jaffa Gate
Standing not far from the Citadel and Tower of David, in between the Jaffa Gate and the Zion Gate, the Kishle is approached via the bustling Omar Ibn Khattab Square. Built in 1837, it was originally a Turkish prison, barracks and police station. Later, it was taken over by the British Mandatory Police who used to confine many of the Jewish underground fighters in the cells. The square is now ringed with souvenir shops and restaurants. There is also a small post office. Street vendors hawk a variety of baked goods, the most common of which is the soft, salty bagel-style roll.

LIONS' GATE
east Old City
Situated in the eastern ramparts of the city wall, the gate takes its name from the lions carved in stone on either side of the opening. The lion, which is the symbol of Jerusalem and appears on the city standard, was in an earlier era the symbol of the Egyptian Mamluk ruler Beybars, who reigned in the second half of the 13th century. The gate is also known as St Stephen's Gate, in honour of the Christian martyr stoned to death near by, and Bab Sitt Mariam, in memory of Mary, Mother of Christ, who is buried not far from the Gate and, according to some, was born just inside it.

MISGAV LADACH
Jewish Quarter
The street name commemorates the most strategically important of the Jewish hospitals, Misgav Ladach, which was founded in 1879 on the ruins of the 1854 Rothschild Hospital. During the War of Independence, Misgav Ladach hospital tended to the needs of the wounded and was also utilised as a stronghold by the Israeli fighters. The hospital, which contained a synagogue and an important library which had previously belonged to Hezekiah Medini, Chief Rabbi of Hebron, was destroyed during the war. The ruins were restored after the reunification of the city. Jewish soldiers who fell in battle here in the final resistance against the Arab Legion were buried where they had fallen and, after the Six Days War, their remains were re-interred on the Mount of Olives, the holiest of Jewish burial places. After the war, Rothschild House was rebuilt.

MOSQUE OF OMAR
just south of the Church of the Holy Sepulchre
Named in memory of Caliph Omar, who prayed to Jesus outside the Church of the Holy Sepulchre following the conquest of Jerusalem in 638, the Mosque of Omar is frequently confused with the Dome of the Rock. The Mosque of Omar was constructed in the 12th century; the second of its two minarets was put up in the 15th century.

MOUNT ZION
southwest of the Old City
Zion, since Biblical times, has been synonymous with Jerusalem. In the Jewish religion, it has always been considered as enjoying divine protection. It is so integral to Jewish heritage and tradition, that when the concept of Jewish nationhood was revived in Europe in the second half of the 19th century, the people belonging to the movement which grew out of that concept called themselves Zionists. From a Christian standpoint Mount Zion is significant as the site of the Last Supper (see **Coenaculum**), the place where Jesus washed the feet of his disciples and the place where Mary fell into her final sleep (see **Dormition Abbey**).
Buses: 13, 20, 23

◆◆◆
MUSLIM QUARTER
northeast Old City

The largest of all the quarters in the Old City, the Muslim Quarter is a city within a city with residential sections, bazaars, workshops, small factories, restaurants, vegetable markets and religious and educational institutions. Several of the buildings constructed by the Muslim community between the 13th and 16th centuries still stand today. The markets in the Muslim Quarter date back in some cases to the Roman period. The spice market is a gourmet's delight, and fabric and clothing are sold in what is still referred to as the goldsmith's market. Some vendors stock the style of jewellery typical of the Middle East—coin and chain combinations fashioned into belts, necklaces, bracelets and earrings, and beaten metal pendants set with large stones and festooned by chains and coins at the base. For the souvenir hunter there are also exquisite backgammon and chess sets in which the boards are inlaid with mother-of-pearl. The markets are all closely linked and well-lit, in sharp contrast to some of the residential areas in which the houses are set in dark, vaulted tunnels. There are doorways at fairly close intervals in these tunnels, behind which are people's homes, but nothing about the external façade suggests to the Western visitor that this is indeed a residential area. Numerous establishments sell different kinds of refreshments: a strong brew of

Some of the younger residents of the Muslim quarter

Turkish coffee served in tiny cups; full-flavoured tea served in glasses in which mint leaves drape over the rim; hot *pita* bread sprinkled with spices or accompanied by sharply seasoned dips; fresh vegetable salads cut into the tiniest of cubes; or treacly cakes which are generally too sweet for the Western palate. There are also restaurants serving meat dishes.
Buses: 12, 27, 43, 45

NEW GATE
northwest Old City
Seeking to connect the Christian Quarter of the Old City with the Notre Dame Hospice, which is outside the walls, the French Government made several presentations to the Turkish Sultan Abdul-Hamid II. In 1889 he obliged and ordered the construction of the New Gate.

OPHEL ARCHAEOLOGICAL GARDEN
The garden is part of the Western (or Wailing) Wall excavations initiated in 1968 by the Society for the Exploration of the Land of Israel and its Antiquities. Excavations have unearthed finds from different civilisations going back all the way to Solomon. A guided tour of the Ophel Garden excavations is included in a walk along the Old City Walls, on the section from Zion Gate to Dung Gate (entrance from Zion Gate only). See 'Ramparts Walk' below for schedules.
Open: Fridays 9:00 A.M.–3:00 P.M.; Sunday to Thursday 9:00 A.M.–5:00 P.M..
Buses: 1, 38

RAMBAN SYNAGOGUE
Jewish Quarter
The oldest synagogue in the Jewish Quarter, this was built in the second half of the 13th century. Before this there were few Jews in the town, and it was quite difficult to get together the required quorum of ten men, the minimum number for a Jewish prayer meeting. After the synagogue was established, more Jews came to make their homes in the Old City and to pray at the only Jewish house of worship.

The Old City walls: a path runs all the way round

RAMPARTS WALK
This requires quite a lot of time, but it is an exhilarating experience. There are paved paths on top of the city walls with guard rails to ensure the safety of visitors. Staircases at strategic points facilitate access to the ramparts. The total distance around the walls is approximately 2-1/2 miles (4km). With stops and starts and ascent and descent on staircases, the walk should take somewhere

between three and four hours. For families with children, this is a marvellous means of harnessing youthful energy and enthusiasm.
Open: Sunday to Thursday 9.00 A.M.–5:00 P.M.; Fridays and holidays until 3:00 P.M. The section between the Citadel and Zion Gate is open until 9:30 P.M.
Buses: 1, 19, 20, 38.

◆
ST MARK'S CHURCH
Armenian Quarter
Belonging to the Syrian Orthodox Christians, St Mark's is a 12th-century structure built on the foundations of an earlier Byzantine church. It is believed that the site was once that of the home of Mary, the mother of the Apostle Mark. The site is also believed to be the place where Mary, mother of Christ was baptised. St Luke is said to have been the artist whose hand captured her likeness in an antique painting on the southern wall of the church.
Open: daily except Sundays, 9.00 A.M.–noon/3:30/6:00 P.M.

◆◆◆
TEMPLE MOUNT
east Old City
Sacred to Jews, Christians and Muslims, the Temple Mount, in the east of the Old City, is known in Arabic as **Haram esh Sharif** (the noble sanctuary) and in Hebrew as **Har Habayit** (the mountain of the House). The House in question was Solomon's Temple, construction of which began in 960BC. The site was chosen for historical reasons. This was the scene of the

supreme test imposed by God on Abraham, the Patriarch of the Jewish People. Here, on Mount Moriah, Abraham was prepared to sacrifice his son Isaac to the Lord. The slopes of the mountain were very steep, but both Solomon and, after him, Herod changed the topography and turned the area into a wide, flat space. Solomon's Temple was plundered on many occasions, and in 587BC it was destroyed. Following the return from the Babylonian exile, a Second Temple was built in 521BC. This Temple was also plundered and defiled. It was recaptured by the Maccabeans in 165BC. They purified it and resumed the customs and traditions of old. When Herod came to the throne in 37BC, he embellished the structure and made it far grander than it had been before. Five years after its completion, in AD70, Herod's magnificent Temple was razed to the ground by the Romans under the command of Titus. Not content with the destruction of the Temple, Emperor Hadrian ordered that all of Jerusalem be destroyed. In place of Herod's Temple, Hadrian put up a pagan temple to Jupiter. During the Byzantine period, when Jerusalem came under Christian rule, the Jupiter Temple was also destroyed. When Caliph Omar conquered Jerusalem in 638, the Temple Mount became identified with Mohammed. According to the Koran, it was from here that Mohammed ascended to heaven. While Omar remained in power, Jerusalem became recognised as a Muslim religious centre.

The breathtaking **Dome of the Rock** (see page 24) was constructed in 691 by Caliph Abd-el-Malik. The **El Aqsa Mosque** (see page 26) was erected by his son El-Walid to commemorate Mohammed's night journey to heaven. Under the Crusaders, the Dome of the Rock was converted into a church, and the mosque, before it, too, was converted into a church, served first as a residential centre for Crusader kings. Jerusalem again became a Muslim centre in 1187 when the city was conquered by Saladin. In 1867, when Jerusalem was under Ottoman rule, non-Muslims were denied entry to the area. But during the period of the British Mandate, this ban applied only to Jews. Since the Six Days War, a group of Jews intent on praying where their hallowed Temple once stood, have been the cause of numerous imbroglios.

The Dome of the Rock: in the centre of the shrine is the rock from which Mohammed ascended into heaven

TIF'ERET YISRA'EL SYNAGOGUE
Jewish Quarter
Sometimes called the Nissim Bak synagogue in memory of the congregational leader whose initiative led to its construction, the Tif'eret Yisra'el Synagogue was built in the second half of the 19th century. There were insufficient funds to complete it. When the Austrian Emperor Franz Joseph visited Jerusalem and saw the synagogue without a dome, he asked where the roof was. The reply was that the synagogue, like everyone else in Jerusalem, had doffed its hat to the emperor. The message was not lost and he arranged for the community to receive the assistance it required to complete the building.

*According to tradition, David's
tomb lies beneath the Coenaculum*

◆
TOMB OF DAVID
Mount Zion

There is no proof positive that
the grave, located in the same
building complex as the Room of
the Last Supper, is indeed the
final resting place of King David.
The tale, linking the spot with
David's burial site, seems to have
originated in the Middle Ages.
After 1948, Jews, denied access
to other Jewish holy sites in the
Old City, were happy to have
some ancient place of
pilgrimage to call their own, and
turned the Tomb of David into a
shrine. Though it is still the scene
of daily candle-lighting
ceremonies, its importance as a
pilgrim site faded somewhat in
1967 after Jews regained access
to the Western Wall.
Open: Saturday to Thursday
8:00 A.M.–5:00 P.M.; Fridays until
1:00 P.M.

◆◆◆
VIA DOLOROSA
north of Temple Mount

Most Christian pilgrims who come
to Jerusalem retrace the path
along which Christ was forced to
walk with the cross on his back,
on the way to his crucifixion. The
literal translation of Via Dolorosa
is Street of Sorrows—for many
pilgrims, the name is apt,
however, not only because of the
greatest tragedy in the history of
Christianity, but also because of
the spiritual let-down which they
experience. Expectations of
what they will see and
experience along the route of
the Fourteen Stations of the
Cross, are greatly magnified in
their minds, but when pilgrims
come across the bustling Arab
bazaars, the flow of human traffic
and the absence of a hallowed
aura, they are very
disappointed. Yet for those who
stop to look closely at their
surroundings, there is much to
see.

The tradition of following in the
footsteps of Christ began in the
4th century. Originally, there
were only seven stations of the
Cross, but over the years the

number doubled. The original route was from Gethsemane to the Golgotha. The pilgrims made their way via the Qidron Valley. A different route was devised in the 13th century, and the route which is currently taken was fixed in the 19th century. One can walk alone or join a procession. You may join the Franciscan Fathers' procession every Friday at 3:00 P.M. beginning from the Tower of Antonia, near the Lions' Gate (the First Station of the Cross). The street sign for the Via Dolorosa is very clearly marked in Latin capitals as well as in Hebrew and Arabic. It has been transliterated, not translated, so the visitor who cannot find his or her way can say 'Via Dolorosa' to any local and be sure of being pointed in the right direction. *Buses:* 23, 27 to Damascus Gate

The First Station Legend has it that this is where Jesus was condemned to death by the Roman governor Pontius Pilate.

The Second Station Cross the road from the Omariya school to the **Church of the Flagellation**, where Jesus was beaten by Roman soldiers. The church belongs to the Franciscans. Just a little further on is **The Church of the Condemnation of the Cross**,

where there are large paintings depicting the condemnation and the death of Christ. Moving in the direction of the Third Station, the visitor will pass beneath **Ecce Homo Arch**, where Pilate, after presenting Jesus to the crowd in the immediate aftermath of the flagellation, said 'Ecce Homo'—'Behold the man'. **The Ecce Homo Church** is run by the French Sisters of Zion, who provide guided tours. The Sisters of Zion are very well thought of in all spheres of Jerusalem society for their sterling contribution to coexistence and mutual understanding. **The Convent of the Sisters of Zion** was built in 1858 by Father Alphonse Ratisbone, a convert from Judaism. Very close to the Sisters of Zion convent is the **Franciscan School for Biblical Studies**, which boasts an excellent library and archaeological museum. West of the convent of the Sisters of Zion is a series of grottoes owned by the Greek Orthodox Church. One of these grottoes is believed to have been the **Prison of Christ**. On the way to the Third Station, on the corner of Hagai Street, is the **Austrian Hospice**, reputed to have been the first hotel in Jerusalem. For a long period, it served as a hospital, and was again turned into a hotel in 1985.

The Third Station Just across the road from the Austrian Hospice is the Third Station, where Jesus is said to have fallen under the burden of the weight of the cross. In 1856, the site was acquired by the Armenian Catholic Church, which built its own chapel here. There is also a small museum with exhibits mainly from the Second Temple period.

The Fourth Station Distinguished by the Armenian **Church of Our Lady of the Spasm**, this is the spot where Jesus met his mother. The prints of two sandals in the crypt of the church are said to be those of Mary as she stood waiting to catch a glimpse of her son on his way to the crucifixion. Built in 1881, the church stands on the ruins of the Byzantine Church of St Sophia.

The Fifth Station Turning right from Hagai Street into the Via Dolorosa, the visitor may notice a handprint on the wall of the first house on the left. According to tradition, the print is that of the hand of Christ, made when he leaned against the wall to brace himself against the weight of the cross. A Franciscan chapel, built here in 1895, is named in memory of Simon of Cyrene, whom the Romans forced to help Jesus carry the cross.

The Sixth Station Though not mentioned in the gospels, St Veronica is believed to have been the woman who stepped forward from the crowd to wipe blood and grime from the face of Christ. A true imprint of his likeness was said to have been left on her handkerchief, which is today kept in St Peter's in Rome. A Greek Catholic church was built on the site in 1885.

The Seventh Station It was here that Jesus fell for the second time in the course of his fateful journey. The place at the Bet Habad Street intersection is marked by a small Franciscan chapel which is also used by the Catholic Copts. A granite pillar on the site is believed to have been one of the supports for the **Gate of Judgement** on which the names of the accused and the sentences meted out to them were posted.

The Eighth Station A stone to the left bears a Latin Cross and the Greek inscription NIKA, meaning Jesus Christ Conquers. Tradition states that Christ stopped here momentarily to speak to the grieving women of Jerusalem. His words are recorded in Luke 23:27, 'Daughters of Jerusalem, do not weep for me, but weep rather for yourselves and your children.' The route continues in the direction of the Church of the Holy Sepulchre. South of the market is a turn-off into Hatsaba'im Street and the Russian Orthodox **Church of Alexander**.

The Ninth Station This is reached via a flight of steps leading from the bazaar to the Coptic Patriarchate. Here, Jesus stumbled for the third time under the weight of the cross. The compound surrounding the ninth station has been inhabited by Ethiopian monks, maintaining a roof-top monastery, since the 17th century. The roof-top's sovereignty has long been a cause of dispute between the Ethiopians and the Copts.

The remaining five stations are inside the **Church of the Holy Sepulchre**. The **Tenth Station** is the place where Christ was nailed to the cross. **The Eleventh Station** is the scene of the actual crucifixion. Pilgrims who kneel here can feel the slight indentation in the ground where the cross was mounted. **The Twelfth Station**, in a hall belonging to the Greek Orthodox Church, marks the place of Christ's death. **The Thirteenth Station**, located between the 11th and 12th stations, is the place where Mary took Jesus in her arms after he was brought down from the cross. **The Fourteenth Station**, the last station, is where Jesus' body was laid in the tomb. It is reached by descending from Calvary, in the northeast corner, to the centre of a large rotunda,

beneath which is the tomb. It is quite disarming to consider how much the events which took place on this relatively small expanse influenced the destiny of the world.

◆◆◆
WESTERN WALL (WAILING WALL)
Jewish Quarter
One of three walls surrounding the Temple Mount, the Western Wall has survived the ravages of time and war. The outer wall of the Second Temple, it has, in the absence of the Temple itself, become a place of pilgrimage and prayer. To Jews all over the world, it is recognised as the holiest of sites, so much so that some believe that this is where they must come in order that

Solitary worship at the Western Wall, a place of deepest significance to the Jewish people

God may listen to their supplications. The crevices in the wall are filled with thousands of petitions from worshippers asking for good fortune, recovery from an illness, a good marriage partner for a son or a daughter, the gift of a child . . . To parallel the number of Christian denominations represented along the Via Dolorosa, the Western Wall has numerous Jewish services taking place simultaneously, conducted by groups of varying ethnic backgrounds or degrees of belief. A partition divides the men's section from the women's section.

Many Jewish families from abroad come here for their bar mitzvah celebrations (the ceremony marking a Jewish boy's reaching of the age of maturity). Israeli families who cannot afford the expense of a lavish bar mitzvah celebration often choose the Western Wall as their venue. The plaza in front of the wall is never totally deserted: some people come to pray in the pre-dawn hours; newly married brides and grooms, still dressed in their wedding finery, make a practice of praying at the wall soon after tying the knot; many events of national importance are also held at the site. On Sabbath and Jewish festivals, the area is always full. Although begging is forbidden by law, beggars flock here in their droves and can be very tiresome.

Numerous excavations have been and are being carried out in the Western Wall area. Most are open to the public.
Bus: 1

YOHANAN BEN ZAKKAY SYNAGOGUE
Jewish Quarter

This is the largest of four restored Sephardic synagogues. Built early in the 17th century, it was used by the Jordanians as a glorified shelter for sheep and goats. Restoration work on the elaborate structure began soon after the reunification of Jerusalem.

ZEDEKIAH'S CAVE
between Damascus Gate and Herod's Gate

According to legend, King Zedekiah, nearly six centuries before the Christian era, took a route via the caves on his flight from the Babylonians. The area is also known as Solomon's Quarries, because it is believed that the huge stone blocks utilised in the building of the First Temple were hewn at this site.
Open: Sunday to Friday 9:00 A.M.–5:00 P.M.
Buses: 23, 27

ZION GATE
south Old City

More or less the dividing line between the Armenian and Jewish Quarters, the Zion Gate is of significance in the modern history of Israel in that it was through this opening in the walls that the last Jewish survivors of the siege of the 1948 war exited from the Old City to West Jerusalem. The gate was then sealed and remained so until June 1967 when the Old City was taken by Israeli forces.

East Jerusalem—Beyond the Walls

Part of this panoramic sprawl around the old city walls is distinctly Arab in character—despite the modernisation of nearly all the shops in Salah-ed-Din street. Many passers-by are dressed in traditional Middle Eastern garb, the aroma that wafts out of the spice shops can be easily identified with the region, and groups of unemployed men sit in doorways drinking thick coffee or mint-flavoured tea and playing backgammon. In the Middle East, backgammon is called *shesh-besh*. The game goes much faster than it does in the West, and often draws small crowds of spectators. The players usually sit on small rattan stools on either side of a large, tooled metal tray. The tray holds both the backgammon board and the coffee cups.

For Museums, see pages 60–67.

◆◆◆
AMERICAN COLONY HOTEL
Nablus Road

Political ups and downs have minimal effect on the American Colony Hotel, an East Jerusalem fixture belonging to the Spafford family, whose American forebears settled in Jerusalem in the 19th century. The Spaffords brought a group of American Presbyterians over to Jerusalem to engage in good works and the members of the Colony acquired an elegant house which became the nucleus of what is now the modern American Colony Hotel. A permanent exhibition tracing the history of Jerusalem from the end of the 19th century can be viewed in the hotel's public areas. International public figures who visit Jerusalem conduct most of their meetings

Just beyond the walls lies Gethsemane, whose chief feature is the Church of all Nations (below)

with Palestinian leaders at the American Colony Hotel, a place understandably favoured by international news reporters as a home-away-from-home.

Christian graves in the World War I cemetery on Mount Scopus

AMMUNITION HILL
Eshkol Boulevard
The scene of a hard-fought battle between the Israelis and the Jordanians in the June 1967 war, Ammunition Hill, known in Hebrew as Giv'at Hatahmoshet, was one of the important fortifications of the Jordanian Army. After the war, the hill was consecrated as a monument to soldiers who fell in battle.
This is a marvellous place for children to let off steam without doing any damage.
Open: Sunday to Thursday 9:00 A.M.–4:00 P.M.; Fridays until 1:00 P.M.
Buses: 4, 9, 25, 26, 28, 29

BRIGHAM YOUNG UNIVERSITY
between Mount of Olives and Mount Scopus
Primarily of interest to members of the Mormon faith, this impressive campus caused a great deal of controversy when construction began in 1980. Christian missionary activity is forbidden in Israel by law and there were fears about the Mormons' involvement in missionary work. Despite strong opposition by religious Jewish elements, the building was completed and the Mormon presence firmly established.

COMMONWEALTH WAR GRAVES CEMETERY
Mount Scopus
Virtually next door to the Hadassah Hospital is the immaculately maintained Commonwealth War Graves cemetery in which soldiers from British Commonwealth countries who died in World War I remain comrades in their final resting place. The headstones of Christian soldiers are marked with a cross and those of Jewish soldiers with a Star of David. In April, each year, the Australian Embassy conducts its ANZAC day memorial services here, taking care to invite members of the Turkish diplomatic corps. The symbolic gesture of friendship by representatives of countries which were once at war is designed to serve as an example to the Middle East.

HADASSAH HOSPITAL
Mount Scopus
The Hadassah Hospital first opened in 1925. When access to the hospital was obstructed in the wake of the 1948 war, the Hadassah women's Zionist Organisation of America established medical facilities in

other parts of Jerusalem, but re-opened the original Hadassah Hospital following the Six Days War in 1967.
Tours: on request

HEBREW UNIVERSITY
Mount Scopus
This is a must on the agenda of any visitor to Jerusalem. The original campus was inaugurated in 1925 on land which belonged to a distinguished Englishman, Sir John Grey, who agreed to sell it to the World Zionist Organisation. Following the 1948 war, Mount Scopus remained an Israeli enclave in Jordanian territory. It was impossible, under such dangerous circumstances, for the university to continue functioning on the site. A second campus was developed in Giv'at Ram, not far from the entrance to Jerusalem (see page 51). After the Six Days War in 1967, Mount Scopus again became the main campus. It was

restored and enlarged.
Today, it is almost an academic village with magnificent views across the city and towards the Judean Desert, the Dead Sea and Moab mountains. Because of its many and varied sophisticated facilities, it is the scene of numerous international congresses and conventions, not all of which are initiated by the University itself.
Tours are conducted daily at 9:00 A.M. and 11:00 A.M.
Buses: 4, 9, 26, 28

MOUNT OF OLIVES
First mentioned in the Bible in Samuel II, 15:30, the Mount of Olives is of great importance to Jews, Christians and Muslims. In ancient times, it was covered with olive trees. Today, there are few trees, but many shrines. For Jews the Mount of Olives has

The Mount of Olives gives the visitor a good view of the Old City

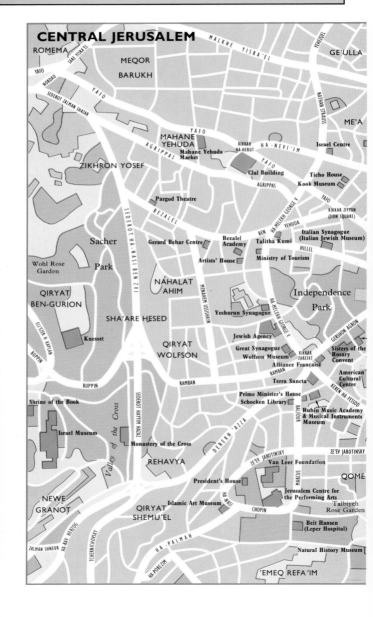

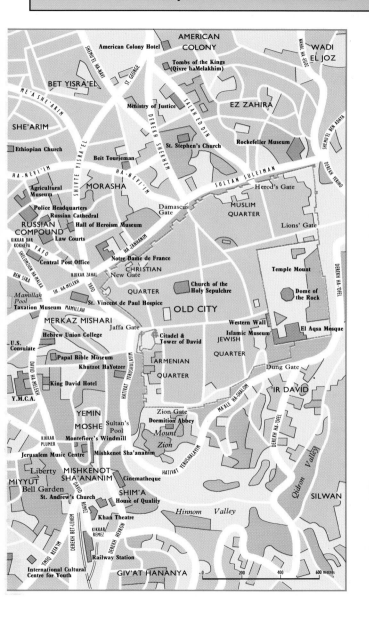

AMERICAN COLONY

WADI EL JOZ

NAHAL HA-EGOZ

American Colony Hotel

SHEMU'EL HA-NAVI

ST. GEORGE

BET YISRA'EL

Tombs of the Kings (Qivre haMelakhim)

EZ ZAHIRA

ME'A SHE'ARIM

Ministry of Justice

SALHED DIN

SHE'ARIM

DEREKH SHEKHEM

SHEMU'EL BEN ADAYA

Ethiopian Church

St. Stephen's Church

Rockefeller Museum

DEREKH YERIHO

Beit Tourjeman

HA-NEVI'IM

HA-NEVI'IM

SULTAN SULEIMAN

Herod's Gate

Agricultural Museum

SHIVTE YISRA'EL

MORASHA

MUSLIM QUARTER

Police Headquarters

Damascus Gate

Russian Cathedral

Lions' Gate

RUSSIAN COMPOUND

Hall of Heroism Museum

KIKKAR BAR KOKHEVA

Law Courts

HA-ZANHANIM

Central Post Office

YAFO

SHLOMZION HA-MALKA

Notre Dame de France

DEREKH HA-'OFEL

BEN SIRA

SH. HA-MELEKH

KIKKAR ZAHAL

New Gate

CHRISTIAN

Temple Mount

Mamillah Pool

YAFO

QUARTER

Dome of the Rock

Taxation Museum

MAMILLAH

St. Vincent de Paul Hospice

Church of the Holy Sepulchre

OLD CITY

MERKAZ MISHARI

Jaffa Gate

Western Wall

Islamic Museum

El Aqsa Mosque

U.S. Consulate

Hebrew Union College

Citadel & Tower of David

JEWISH

DEREKH HA-'OFEL

Papal Bible Museum

HATIVAT YERUSHALAYIM

ARMENIAN

QUARTER

Dung Gate

IR DAVID

Khutzot HaYotzer

King David Hotel

DAVID HA-MELEKH

Y.M.C.A.

YEMIN

Zion Gate

MA'ALE HA-SHALOM

MOSHE

Sultan's Pool

Dormition Abbey

DEREKH HA-'OFEL

Montefiore's Windmill

Mishkenot Sha'ananim

Mount Zion

KIKKAR PLUMER

Jerusalem Music Centre

HATIVAT YERUSHALAYIM

Qidron Valley

Liberty

MISHKENOT SHA'ANANIM

Cinematheque

MIYYUT

DAVID

Bell Garden

St. Andrew's Church

SHIM'A

House of Quality

Hinnom Valley

SILWAN

KEREN

Khan Theatre

DEREKH BET-LEHEM

KIKKAR REMEZ

DEREKH HEVRON

TMOL REGA'IM

Railway Station

International Cultural Centre for Youth

GIV'AT HANANYA

0   200   400   600 metres

EAST JERUSALEM – BEYOND THE WALLS

A 'ship of the desert' waits patiently outside the Tomb of the Virgin Mary on the Mount of Olives

always been the most sacred of burial grounds, and even today, the most pious Jews, including those living abroad, leave a request in their wills that they be buried on the Mount of Olives. Jews believe that when Messianic redemption finally comes, the Messiah will enter the city from the Mount of Olives through the Golden Gate, otherwise known as the Gate of Repentance.

The manifold Christian shrines on the Mount of Olives mark the places where Christ spent his last days before being taken into captivity. The New Testament books of Mark and Luke record his sojourn with friends in the village of **Bethany**. It was on the Mount of Olives that he spoke to his disciples, predicted the

destruction of Jerusalem and foresaw his own fate. He was subsequently arrested in the **Garden of Gethsemane**, at the foot of the Mount of Olives. It was also from the Mount of Olives that the Ascension of Christ took place.

Many visitors begin their tour of the Mount of Olives on the roadway between the Seven Arches Hotel and the Jewish Cemetery. From here, the view of the Temple Mount is quite breathtaking. Arab souvenir-hawkers line the road and there is always at least one man with a camel who takes a small fee from tourists who want to be photographed sitting astride the 'ship of the desert'.

Christian sites on the Mount of Olives include the **Church of the Ascension**, the **Church of Pater Noster, St Mary's Tomb** (the **Church of the Assumption**), the Russian **Church of Mary**

Magdalene, the **Church of All Nations**, otherwise known as the **Church of Agony at Gethsemane**, and the **Dominus Flevit Church**.

Each of these churches is built in its own individual architectural style. The most distinctive is the Church of All Nations, whose artistic façade contains a plethora of statues and paintings depicting the last agonies of Christ. The Russian churches are identified by the onion-head domes which stand out against the skyline. For one of the most memorable views of the country, those who have the stamina should climb the 214 steps to the bell-tower of the Russian Church of the Ascension. It is certainly well worth the effort.

Pilgrim groups can be found daily in the area, and it is quite easy for the individual visitor to get within earshot of the guides to hear of the history and traditions related to each of the sites.

Visitors who are not up to walking from one church to another can catch a brief glimpse of some of them from the Route 99 tour bus.

TOMBS OF THE KINGS
near corner of Nablus Road and Salah-ed-Din Street
Once believed to be the tombs of ancient Kings of Israel, these impressive underground tombs were in fact hewn into the rock on the orders of the Mesopotamian Queen Helene. Bring a flashlight.
Open: Monday to Friday 8:30 A.M.–1:00 P.M.
Buses: 23, 27

West Jerusalem—The New City
If you have only a short time in Jerusalem, you will want to spend it in East Jerusalem, the older part of the city, but there are some interesting places to visit in West, or 'downtown', Jerusalem and this is the area to go for the fashionable shops and a big choice of restaurants and cafés of all sorts.

For Museums, see pages 60–67.

ALLIANCE FRANÇAISE
(Gershon Agron, near Keren HaYessod intersection
The Alliance Française has a library, concerts and poetry readings and a dairy restaurant specialising in crêpes.

◆
AMERICAN CULTURAL CENTRE
19a Keren HaYessod Street
Although American newspapers and magazines are readily available in Israel, they are very expensive. Some Americans visiting or residing in Israel have discovered that it is infinitely preferable to go to the American Cultural Centre, where they can also see videos of American sports, news and documentaries. A gym and body-building studio operated by an American is in the basement. At ground level is a book and gift store specialising in Jerusalem souvenirs.
Buses: 4, 7, 14, 48

◆
ARTS AND CRAFTS LANE
Khutzot HaYotzer
Sandwiched between Yemin Moshe, the terraced

neighbourhood adjacent to Montefiore's Windmill, and the wall surrounding the Old City, the arts and crafts lane houses numerous galleries and studios. The artists and craftsmen work here in studio shops and sell directly to the public.
Open: the studios open at 10:00 A.M. and most stay open till 6:00 P.M. on Thursdays and till 2:00 P.M. on Fridays. On Saturday nights they are open from 8:30 P.M.–11:30 P.M. and in the summer months they are also open on Tuesday night.

◆◆
BEZALEL
west of HaMelekh George V (King George) Street
Conveniently situated in downtown Jerusalem, less than five minutes' walk away from the main commercial centre, the **Bezalel Academy of Art and Design** at 1 Bezalel Street (near the Ben Yehuda/King George Street intersection, behind the Ministry of Tourism), is the cradle of Israel's artistic endeavour.
Around the corner is **Artists' House**. The imposing building at 10–12 Shemu'el haNagid Street holds regular exhibitions and there are other programmes for visitors. There is a restaurant and bar.
Buses: 4, 7, 9, 17, 19
A curving sweep of a street, Shemu'el haNagid leads north towards to the Ben Yehuda/King George Street intersection and to Mesilat Yesharim Street at the back of the **Hamashbir department store**. Mesilat Yesharim in turn intersects with Agrippas to the north, the rear

section of the MAHANE YEHUDA MARKET, which offers a vast selection of low priced Middle Eastern eateries as well as shopping opportunities.

The Shrine of the Book houses the unique collection of ancient Dead Sea Scrolls

◆◆
DEAD SEA SCROLLS
The Shrine of the Book, Israel Museum, Ruppin Street
Discovered in 1947 by Bedouin shepherds in the Qumran caves in the Judean desert, the scrolls recording the Jewish uprising against the Romans in AD132–135, as well as fragments from books of the Bible, are housed in The Shrine of the Book, whose architectural concept is based on the shape of the ancient clay vessels in which the scrolls were stored. (The Shrine of the Book is part of the Israel Museum complex, see under **Museums**.)

'EMEQ REFA'IM
Retaining its Biblical name, 'Emeq Refa'im, or the Valley of Ghosts, is the main street of a neighbourhood known as the German Colony. It was here that the Philistines were defeated by David. The first contemporary settlers, if they can be so designated, were a group of South German Protestants known as Templars, who had come to set up an agricultural colony. The first house in the German Colony went up in 1873. In World War II, the British evacuated all the Germans and turned the area into a security zone, but, following Israel's independence in 1948, many new immigrants moved into the German Colony and the stately houses, including those built by wealthy Arabs, were converted into apartment-style dwellings.
Buses: 4, 14, 18, 24

'EN KEREM
southeast of Mount Herzl
To most Israelis the immediate association with the former Arab village of 'En Kerem is the **Hadassah-Hebrew University Medical Centre** with its famed Chagall windows (see separate entry). But 'En Kerem also has many biblical and cultural connotations. It has become the scene not only for the visual arts but also the performing arts. From a biblical perspective, 'En Kerem, which means Spring of the Vineyard, is believed to be the birthplace of John the Baptist. The **Church of John the Baptist** belongs to the Spanish Franciscan Order. There is also

a 130-year-old convent maintained by the Sisters of Zion. This is in addition to their convent, hospice and study centre in the Old City. Near the convent is a **Russian Church** and the **Church of the Visitation**. The latter is close to **Mary's Well**, otherwise known as the Spring of the Virgin. Legend has it that this place was the summer home of Zachariya and Elisheva, the parents of John the Baptist. It was here that the pregnant Elisheva was visited by Mary, mother of Christ in her flight from Nazareth.
'En Kerem, which also has restaurants and coffee shops, seems to be a long way from the city proper. In fact, it is only 15–20 minutes by bus. The clean air and the tranquil atmosphere together with the spectacular view, make it a journey worth taking.
Buses: For the suburb, 17; to include Hadassah Hospital 19, 27

ETHIOPIAN CHURCH
Ethiopia Street
Ethiopians have lived continuously in the Christian Quarter of the Old City of Jerusalem since the 7th century. They have lived outside the walls of the Old City for just over a hundred years. The street in which their ornate church was built used to enjoy the reputation of being one of the more exclusive streets in Jerusalem and contains several elegant buildings. The Ethiopian Church stands diagonally across the road from the British Council Library.
Buses: nearest are 3, 4, 9, 11, 29, 40

JERUSALEM ENVIRONS

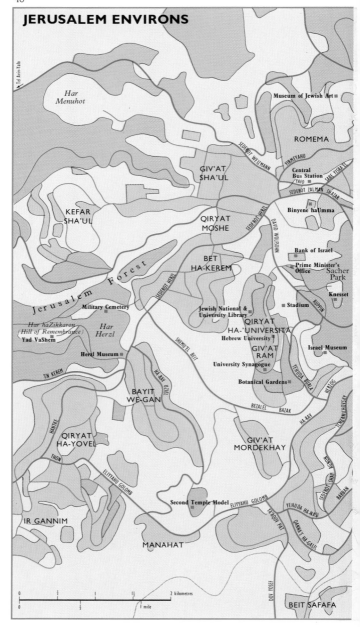

Har Menuhot

Museum of Jewish Art ■

ROMEMA

SEDEROT WEIZMANN

YIRMEYAHU

GIV'AT SHA'UL

Central Bus Station
YAFO

SARE YISRA'EL

SEDEROT ZALMAN SHAZAR

KEFAR SHA'UL

QIRYAT MOSHE

SEDEROT HERZL

Binyene haUmma ■

DAVID WOLFSON

BET HA-KEREM

Bank of Israel ■

■ Prime Minister's Office

Sacher Park

Knesset ■

Jerusalem Forest

SEDEROT HERZL

Military Cemetery ■

Jewish National & University Library ■

■ Stadium

RUPPIN

Har haZikkaron (Hill of Remembrance)
Yad VaShem

Har Herzl

QIRYAT HA-'UNIVERSITA

Hebrew University ¶

Israel Museum ■

'EN KEREM

Herzl Museum ■

SHEMU'EL BEIT

HA-RAV UZI'EL

GIV'AT RAM

University Synagogue ■

YEHUDA BURLA

HERZOG

Botanical Gardens ■

BAYIT WE-GAN

BEZALEL

BAZAK

HA RAV

TSHERNIKHOVSKY

HANTKE

QIRYAT HA-YOVEL

THON

GIV'AT MORDEKHAY

KOVSHE

SEDEROT USHAN

RABBAN

IR GANNIM

ELIYYAHU GOLOMB

Second Temple Model ■

ELIYYAHU GOLOMB

YA'AKON PAT

YEHUDA HA-NASI

GANNE HA-GALIL

MANAHAT

POLA

BEIT SAFAFA

Tel Aviv-Yafo

0   ¼   ½   1   1½   2 kilometres

0   ½   1 mile

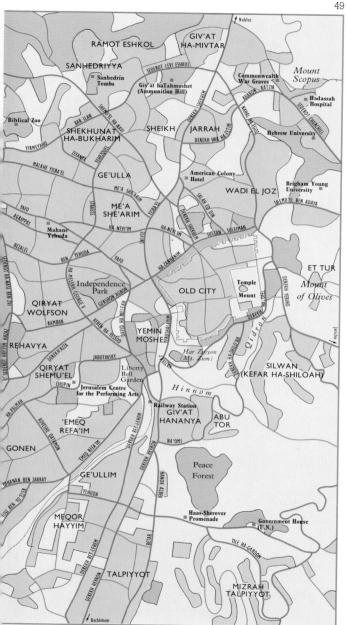

↑ Nablus

RAMOT ESHKOL

GIV'AT HA-MIVTAR

SANHEDRIYYA

SEDEROT LEVI ESHKOL

Sanhedrin Tombs

Commonwealth War Graves

Mount Scopus

Giv'at haTahmoshet (Ammunition Hill)

AHARON KATZIR

NAHAL HA-EGOZ

Hadassah Hospital

Biblical Zoo

BAR ILAN

SHEMU'EL HA-NAVI

DEREKH SHEKHEM

SHEKHUNAT HA-BUKHARIM

SHEIKH

JARRAH

DEREKH HAR HA-ZETIM

Hebrew University

YIRMEYAHU

ZEFANYA

TEODEROSL

SEDEROT CHURCHILL

MALKHE YISRA'EL

GE'ULLA

ME'A SHE'ARIM

American Colony Hotel

WADI EL JOZ

Brigham Young University

YAFO

ME'A SHE'ARIM

YISRA'EL

SALAH ED DIN

SHEMU'EL BEN ADAYA

AGRIPPAS

STRAUSS

HA-NEVI'IM

DEREKH HEVRON

BEZALEL

Mahane Yehuda

YAFO

SHIVTE

SULTAN SULEIMAN

ET TUR

BEN YEHUDA

HA-MELEKH GEORGE V

HA-TAMHUYIM

HA-NEVI'IM

Mount of Olives

Temple Mount

DEREKH YERIHO

Independence Park

GERSHON AGRON

OLD CITY

HA-OZEL

QIRYAT WOLFSON

KEREN HA-YESOD

DAVID HA-MELEKH

DEREKH

HA-SHILOAH

Qidron

↓ Jericho

RAMBAN

REHAVYA

DEREKH AZZA

YEMIN MOSHE

YERUSHALAYIM

SILWAN (KEFAR HA-SHILOAH)

JABOTINSKY

Liberty Bell Garden

Har Ziyyon (Mt. Zion)

QIRYAT SHEMU'EL

CHOPIN

Jerusalem Centre for the Performing Arts

Hinnom

SEDEROT HAYYIM HAZAZ

SEDEROT HA-NASI BEN ZVI

HA-PALMAH

QOSEHE GALANON

Railway Station

GIV'AT HANANYA

ABU TOR

'EMEQ REFA'IM

DEREKH BET-LEHEM

NA'OMI

GONEN

'EMEQ REFA'IM

DEREKH HEVRON

HINNOM

Peace Forest

YOHANAN BEN ZAKKAY

GE'ULLIM

YEHUDA

Haas-Sherover Promenade

Government House (U.N.)

YOEL BEN NO'AH

MEQOR HAYYIM

BETAR

DEREKH BET-LEHEM

'OLE HA-GARDOM

TALPIYYOT

MIZRAH TALPIYYOT

↓ Bethlehem

GREAT SYNAGOGUE
HaMelekh George V (King George Street)

Opened in 1983, the marble and stained-glass edifice in King George Street opposite the Sheraton Plaza hotel is one of the largest synagogues in the country, with a seating capacity for 1,700. It was erected in memory of the six million Jews who perished in the Nazi Holocaust, as well as the soldiers who fell in Israel's wars. The synagogue owes its existence to the late Dr Maurice Jaffe, one of its key officials, who was among the first Jewish clergymen to enter the death camps after World War II. There are actually two houses of worship under one roof—one for Sephardi worshippers and the other for Ashkenazi. A huge plaza in front of the building is often used for outdoor concerts. On important Jewish holidays such as Rosh Hashana, the Jewish New Year and Yom Kippur, the Day of Atonement, the plaza is filled with worshippers taking a break from services.

Buses: 4, 7, 8, 9, 14, Sunday to Friday except Jewish Holidays
Tours: Sunday to Thursday 9:00 A.M.–1:00 P.M.; Friday until noon

◆◆◆
HAAS-SHEROVER PROMENADE

Situated along the stretch of road running from North Talpiot to Armon Hanatziv (Government House), is a truly magnificent promenade offering spectacular views of the Old City and the nearby suburb of Abu Tor, a neighbourhood inhabited by both Jews and Arabs. It can be reached on foot via the Jerusalem Peace Forest. Although this is a really pleasant walk, it is for the most part an uphill climb. An easier way to get there is by bus.

Buses: 8, 48

A climb up the Haas-Sherover Promenade will be rewarded by the views over the Old City

◆◆
HADASSAH-HEBREW UNIVERSITY MEDICAL CENTRE
'En Kerem

When the 1948 war made it impossible for the staff at the original Hadassah Hospital to continue their work, the whole complex on Mount Scopus was evacuated and alternative premises were set up. The hospital has achieved international acclaim by virtue of the fact that it treats patients from neighbouring but hostile Arab countries.

The richly coloured windows by Chagall in the Hadassah Hospital

The Hospital **Synagogue** is of particular interest to visitors from abroad for the 12 world-famous stained-glass windows created by Marc Chagall, depicting scenes from the story of Jacob's 12 sons.
Open: Sunday to Thursday 8:00 A.M.–1:30 P.M., 2:00/3:45 P.M.; Friday 8:00 A.M.–12:45 P.M.
Buses: 19, 27

◆◆◆
HEBREW UNION COLLEGE
13 David haMelekh (King David) Street
A house of worship, a rabbinical seminary, the Skirball archaeological museum (see page 66), a hostel, a social and cultural outlet and a restaurant are all under the umbrella of the beautifully designed Hebrew Union College and Jerusalem Centre of the World Union for Progressive Judaism. The main entrance is via King David Street, some two minutes' walk from the King David Hotel.
Buses: 5, 6, 15, 18, 21, 30

◆◆
HEBREW UNIVERSITY, GIV'AT RAM
After the Hebrew University was evacuated from its original campus on Mount Scopus, its departments were scattered in various parts of West Jerusalem. In 1954, construction began on a new campus in Giv'at Ram, not far from the entrance to the city. Most departments were transferred to this campus in 1958. After the Six Days War and the restoration and expansion of the original campus on Mount Scopus, the departments were again transferred (see Hebrew University, Mount Scopus, page 41). None the less, the Giv'at Ram campus is still very much in use. Among other things, it houses the Jewish National and University Library, a botanical

garden, a large sports stadium and the Open Eye Science Centre (see **Museums**).

The Jewish National Library has the largest collection of Judaica in the world. It is also the largest library in the Middle East.

Library open: 9:00 A.M.–2:00 P.M., Fridays until noon
Buses: 9, 24, 28. Buses 9 and 28 run between the Giv'at Ram campus and the Mount Scopus campus.

HINNOM VALLEY

south of Mount Zion

Many visitors to Jerusalem who know their Bible well use it as a handbook when touring the city. This can often lead to disappointment because every site has undergone many changes in the course of time, and few bear any resemblance to the image conveyed by the Bible. A case in point is the Hinnom Valley, which was first cited in the Book of Joshua. A continuation of the Qidron Valley, it bordered the territories of Benjamin and Judah. In biblical times, the area, which is also known as Gehinnom—the Valley of Hell—served as the main cemetery of Jerusalem. Nowadays, the valley is distinguished primarily as an arts and entertainment centre. Its features include the Arts and Crafts Lane (Khutzot HaYotzer); the Sultan's Pool, a huge outdoor entertainment expanse adjacent to Arts and Crafts Lane; the Jerusalem Cinematheque, which includes a more than passable restaurant with wonderful balcony views; plus the Khan

Theatre, a nightclub and restaurant in what was once a Turkish stable and inn. All these facilities are accessible from Yemin Moshe or Hebron Road.

HOUSE OF QUALITY

12 Hebron Road

The House of Quality, just behind St Andrews Church of Scotland, contains the studios of some of Jerusalem's best artists and artisans. There is also a restaurant, which is one of the most popular folk singing establishments in the city.

Exhibitions/Studios open: Sunday to Thursday 10:00 A.M.–6:00 P.M.; Friday until 1:00 P.M.
Buses: 5, 6, 7, 21

◆

INDEPENDENCE PARK

(HaMelekh George (King George) Street/Agron Street

A large expanse of undulating greenery on the edge of downtown West Jerusalem, Independence Park was for many years the focal point of Israel Independence Day activities in the capital. Nowadays, merry-makers are more inclined to fill the Ben Yehuda Mall and the Liberty Bell Garden. However, Independence Park has remained a popular picnic spot.

◆

JERUSALEM ARTISTS' HOUSE

12 Shemu'el haNagid Street (off Bezalel), West Jerusalem

The restaurant-cum-bar on the ground floor of this stately old building is open till late at night. Exhibitions are held in the various galleries.

Open: daily 10:00 A.M.–6:00 P.M.

The Jerusalem Centre for Performing Arts – venue for ballet, drama, theatre, film and music recitals

JERUSALEM CENTRE FOR PERFORMING ARTS
Marcus/Chopin Streets
The Jerusalem Centre for the Performing Arts is the pivotal point of entertainment in the capital. It is the headquarters of the Israel Festival and its stages have been used for every type of performing arts. In addition, the Jerusalem Theatre also functions as a cinema, conference hall and exhibition hall. There is a variety of restaurants to choose from.
Buses: 15. Also 4, 7, 8, 14, 48 to Laromme Hotel, or 9 to Balfour Road, and short walk.

JEWISH AGENCY
HaMelekh George (King George) Street
For several years prior to the establishment of the State of Israel, the Jewish Agency took on a quasi-governmental role. The World Zionist Organization (WZO) is also based here.
Buses: 4, 7, 8, 9, 17, 19

KING DAVID HOTEL
David haMelekh (King David) Street
Situated opposite the majestic YMCA building, the King David Hotel is the flagship of the local Dan chain of hotels. The hotel was built in 1930 with the design of the lounge reflecting the architectural style of King David's own era. Although there are now more elegant and sophisticated hotels in Jerusalem, the King David has a certain snob appeal, and continues to be the first choice for visiting celebrities. Most State banquets hosted by the Prime Minister are held at the King David; and those hosted by the President, though held at the Presidential residence, are catered by the King David. See also under **Accommodation**.

The symbol of state, outside the Knesset, Israel's Parliament

KNESSET
Ruppin Street

The seat of Israel's Parliament, the Knesset (Assembly) is the focal point of a garden setting on a hill-top area designated for government offices. When Israel achieved independence in 1948, there was no parliamentary structure, and the 120-member legislature used the Jewish Agency building for its early sessions. After occupying temporary premises in Tel Aviv and then Jerusalem, in 1966 the Knesset moved into its present home overlooking Ruppin Road. The construction of the vast complex, much of which is built into the hillside below ground level for protection in the event of an enemy air raid, was financed by the late James Rothschild.

The Knesset's main reception hall is decorated with Chagall tapestries. Across the road from the entrance to the grounds of the building is a huge statue of the symbol of the State—a seven-branched candelabrum into which are carved significant events in Jewish history. Just behind this area is a fenced-off section in which public demonstrations are held. As a democratic country, Israel allows any group of citizens who may have a grievance to demonstrate in front of the Knesset, provided they have a police permit.
Open: Monday to Wednesday during session time
Tours: Sundays and Thursdays 8:30 A.M.–2:30 P.M. Bring passports
Bus: 9, 24, 28

LIBERTY BELL GARDEN
David haMelekh (King David) Street, south

One of the most attractive public gardens in the whole of Israel, the Liberty Bell Garden alongside the Laromme Hotel and facing Yemin Moshe, was dedicated in 1976 in honour of the US Declaration of Independence bicentennial with a replica of Philadelphia's Liberty Bell. There are lawns, well-lit paths, a skating rink, a playground, numerous picnic spots, lots of stone benches, an amphitheatre and a train station. The Liberty Bell Park is often used for outdoor fairs and concerts. The 'Train Theatre' puts on puppet shows for children during the summer.
Buses: 4, 5, 6, 7, 8, 14, 15, 48

A stallholder displays his wares in the Mahane Yehuda market

◆◆◆
MAHANE YEHUDA MARKET
between Yafo (Jaffa) Road and Agrippas Street
Not far from the entrance to the city, the colourful Mahane Yehuda covered market has been operating since 1887. Some stalls are open before the first light of dawn and stay open till after dusk or two hours before sunset on Fridays and the eve of Jewish holy days. The market is busiest on Wednesdays and Thursdays. In addition to fruit and vegetables, the market offers fresh flowers, meat and poultry, dairy products, fish, cakes, cookies, household items, clothing, cosmetics, footwear and toys, and is studded with eateries.
Buses: 6, 7, 8, 11, 18, 20 pass Mahane Yehuda market.

◆◆◆
ME'A SHE'ARIM
between Strauss Street and Shivte Yisra'el Street
No visit to Jerusalem is complete without a leisurely stroll through the Me'a She'arim district. Founded in 1874, it was one of the earliest Jewish settlements outside the walls of the Old City. Translated, its name means One Hundred Gates. To come here is like walking into the past—into the hamlets and villages of pre-war Europe. The only comparable non-Jewish community in the world is the Amish of Pennsylvania, US. The men are nearly all bearded and dressed in black. The women are modestly attired in long-sleeved, high-necked dresses. Those who are married keep their heads covered beneath a turban, head-scarf or wig. Some have radios in their homes, but very few have television sets. Those who do

own a television set usually confine their viewing to video programmes on religious subjects. Most of Me'a She'arim's inhabitants are of Central European origin and adhere to an extraordinary variety of sects within ultra-orthodox Judaism. There are more institutions for study and prayer in this relatively small area than there are anywhere else in the city. Visitors, especially women, should be clad in an inoffensive manner when walking through Me'a She'arim—there are many young fundamentalists who will not hesitate to make life unpleasant for anyone who offends their sensibilities. Also be careful about using your camera. Many of the residents have religious scruples about being photographed. Some will cover their faces with their headgear and scurry away, others will try to grab the camera. Never try to photograph them on the Sabbath.

Me'a She'arim is accessible from Strauss Street at one end and Shivte Yisra'el Street at the other. Don't limit yourself to a walk through the main street alone. There are many fascinating alleyways and courtyards.
Buses: 1, 3, 11, 29. 4, 9 stop nearby

◆◆◆
MISHKENOT SHA'ANANIM
off David haMelekh (King David) Street

Mishkenot Sha'ananim, literally the Dwelling Places of the Tranquil, was the first Jewish housing project outside the Old City walls. The houses were put up by Sir Moses Montefiore with money which he received from American Jewish philanthropist Judah Touro. Montefiore also had the windmill constructed that has since become a city landmark. From 1948 to 1967, Mishkenot Sha'ananim and the adjacent Yemin Moshe neighbourhood were on the edge of no-man's land and were frequently fired upon by Jordanian snipers. Only the poorest of the poor lived here in daily terror of their lives. After the Six Days War, the poor and needy were evacuated, and a massive restoration project in urban renewal and development was undertaken. Many of those who moved into the renewed homes were well-to-do artists who turned their homes into residential studios open to the public. Mishkenot Sha'ananim is now the focal point of many international cultural events. One of its prime assets is the Jerusalem Music Centre, whose concert hall has the best acoustics in the country.

It is very difficult to tell where Mishkenot Sha'ananim ends and where Yemin Moshe begins or vice versa. The whole neighbourhood has a unique style of its own. Its terraced stone cottages nearly all have attractive gardens enclosed by wrought iron fencing. Steep staircases lead from Montefiore's Windmill to the Sultan's Pool and Khutzot HaYotzer. Near the bottom of the main staircase, which is the one directly alongside the windmill, is the Mishkenot Sha'ananim Restaurant, one of the most exclusive in the city.
Buses: 4, 5, 6, 7, 8, 14, 15, 18, 21, 26, 48

MONASTERY OF THE CROSS
Sederot Hayyim Hazaz
This fortress-like structure is set right at the bottom of Rehavya Valley and is not always visible from the main road. Medieval in style, it was built in the 11th century on the foundations of a 5th-century Georgian monastery. The Georgians sold the premises to the Greek Orthodox Church. The Monastery takes its name from the legend that the wood for Christ's cross was cut from timber which grew in the valley.
Open: Monday to Saturday 9:00 A.M.–5:00 P.M.; Friday until 1:30 P.M.
Bus: 19 to Tchernichovsky

◆
MONTEFIORE WINDMILL
See page 63

◆◆◆
MOUNT HERZL
Sederot Herzl
Theodor Herzl was the 19th-century visionary who founded the Zionist Movement for the revival of Jewish nationalist aspirations. His remains are buried on the mountain which bears his name and the site has become a national memorial. The **Herzl Museum** (see under Museums) at the entrance contains many of his archives in a reconstruction of his study. The tombs of many of the leaders of the State and the State-in-the-making are buried here. Mount Herzl is also the site of Israel's main military cemetery and is the scene each year of the launching of the Israel Independence Day celebrations.

A park surrounds the tomb of the founder of Zionism on Mount Herzl

Cemetery open: daily until sunset
Tombs and Museum open: Sunday to Thursday 9:00 A.M.–5:00 P.M.; Friday until 1:00 P.M.
Buses: 17, 18, 20, 23, 27

◆◆◆
NAHALAT SHIVA
near Zion Square
The third Jewish neighbourhood to be built outside the walls of the Old City, Nahalat Shiva is one of the prettiest places in the city. Recently given a face-lift, the area is now a very pleasant shopping centre with a wide choice of dining options in terms of both price and variety.

RUSSIAN COMPOUND

between Yafo (Jaffa) Road, Shivte Yisra'el and Heleni haMalka

In 1853 a portion of land in this area was presented by the Turkish Sultan to the Tsar of Russia and another parcel of land in the same area was purchased by the Russian Consul. A number of buildings were constructed by the Russian Palestine Society to accommodate the vast numbers of Russian pilgrims who flocked to Jerusalem. The Russian Consulate building was also here. The Holy Trinity Cathedral, with its white walls and pale green domes, is the only property here which still remains Russian since the other buildings were purchased from the Soviet government by the Israel authorities. One of the buildings is now the Hall of Heroism Museum (see under **Museums**).

Other buildings are used as police headquarters, prison cells, law courts and offices.
Buses: 3, 5, 6, 18, 19, 20

◆ ST ANDREW'S CHURCH

near Jerusalem Railway Station

Scottish visitors find a little piece of home at St Andrew's Church of Scotland. The beautiful church, set in spacious grounds, was built in 1927 to serve as a memorial to Scottish soldiers who fell in the Battle for Jerusalem during World War I. The church has a comfortable hospice and offers a glorious view of the Hinnom Valley, Mount Zion and the Judean Desert.

◆ SHEKHUNAT HA-BUKHARIM (BUKHARAN QUARTER)

between Zefanya, Yehezqel, Bar Ilan

One of the older neighbourhoods in West Jerusalem, the Bukharan Quarter was, at the turn of the 19th century, one of the most affluent sectors of the city. Founded by wealthy immigrants from Bukhara, Samarkand and Tashkent, it boasted unusually wide streets and luxurious houses built around large courtyards. The fortunes of the founding families took a turn for the worse in the aftermath of the Russian Revolution but the external façades of the buildings still show signs of past grandeur and ongoing restoration efforts may, at some future date, bring the area back to its days of glory. Meanwhile, with the outgrowth of the religious neighbourhoods of Me'a She'arim and Geula, the Bukharan Quarter has adopted a similar identity.
Buses: 4, 9

◆ TALITHA KUMI

HaMelekh George (King George) Street

Near the corner of Ben Yehuda Street, is what looks like the entrance to an old stone building. This is Talitha Kumi—or rather all that remains of this, the first building erected in West Jerusalem in the 1860s.

◆◆◆ YAD VASHEM

Har Hazikkaron

Slightly west of Mount Herzl, Har Hazikkaron, the Hill of Remembrance, serves as the

eternal memorial for the six million Jews who perished in the Nazi Holocaust. Opened in 1957, the site is the scene of the annual memorial service held for Jews who have neither graves nor tombstones.

Yad Vashem has an enormous collection of documents and a permanent photographic exhibition. See also **Museums**.

Yad Vashem: the Ohel Jiskor hall (below), memorial to the dead; in the park (top), poignant sculptures

YMCA
David haMelekh (King David) Street

The West Jerusalem 'Y' (there is also one in East Jerusalem), is more than 100 years old. Aside from its architectural beauty, it should be visited for any number of other reasons. First and foremost, it is a living symbol of ecumenism—Christians, Jews and Muslims use its manifold facilities every day of the week. The Y also has a very fine hostel and a first-class restaurant.
Tower open: Monday to Saturday 9:00 A.M.–2:00 P.M.
Buses: 6, 18

◆◆◆
ZION SQUARE
Yafo (Jaffa) Road/Ben Yehuda

Zion Square, in the very heart of town, is primarily important because it helps visitors to get a sense of their bearings. There are two important landmarks—one is a branch of Bank Leumi and the other a branch of Bank Hapoalim.

Museums

The museums described below are listed alphabetically for the whole of Jerusalem.

Contrary to the practice in most other countries, museums in Israel open at a very early hour, the vast majority by 9:00 A.M. Entry charges vary.
Most of the museums are on the 99 circular bus route. If you buy a two-day ticket for this route, it will save you having to figure out which bus goes where.

AMMUNITION HILL MUSEUM
Levi Eshkol Boulevarde, Ramat Eshkol
Commemorating those who fell in the Six Days War.
Open: Sunday to Thursday 9:00 A.M.–4:00 P.M.; Friday until 1:00 P.M.
Buses: 9, 25, 28

ARMENIAN ART AND HISTORY MUSEUM
Armenian Quarter, Old City
150-year-old museum with frescos, paintings, ritual objects, manuscripts dating from the 7th century; documentation of the slaughter of Armenians by Turks during World War I.
Open: Monday to Saturday 10:00 A.M.–5:00 P.M.
Buses: 3, 13, 19, 20

BURNT HOUSE OF KATHROS
13 Tif'eret Yisra'el Street, Jewish Quarter
Discovered by archaeologists in 1970, the Burnt House was the home of a Jewish family at the end of the Second Temple period in AD70. Sight and Sound presentations 9:30 A.M., 11:30 A.M., 5:30 P.M.
Open: Sunday to Thursday 9:00 A.M.–5:00 P.M.; Friday until 1:00 P.M.
Buses: 1, 38

FRANCISCAN BIBLE MUSEUM CHURCH OF FLAGELLATION
Via Dolorosa, Old City
Centuries-old findings by Franciscan scholars and archaeologists.
Open: Sunday by appointment
Buses: 23, 27

GREEK ORTHODOX PATRIARCHATE MUSEUM
Greek Orthodox Patriarchate Street, Old City
Ceremonial objects from different periods in history as well as archaeological finds.
Open: Monday to Friday 9:00 A.M.–1:00 P.M. and 3:00/5:00 P.M.; Saturday 9.00 A.M.–1:00 P.M.
Buses: 3, 13, 19, 20

HALL OF HEROISM
Russian Compound, Yafo (Jaffa) Road (near Heleni haMalka)
The museum documents the history of various Jewish underground movements.
Open: Sunday to Thursday 9:00 A.M.–3:00 P.M.; Friday 10:00 A.M.–1:00 P.M.
Buses: 3, 5, 6, 18, 19, 20

HERZL MUSEUM
Herzl Boulevarde at the entrance gate to Mount Herzl
The reconstruction of the study of Theodor Herzl, the founder of

the Zionist Movement which brought about the Jewish national renaissance.
Open: Sunday to Thursday 9:00 A.M.–6:30 P.M.; Friday 9:00 A.M.–1:00 P.M.
Buses: 18, 20, 24

ISLAMIC MUSEUM
Temple Mount, Old City
In addition to the exhibits, which are fine examples of Islamic craftsmanship and tradition, the museum offers a fascinating view of architectural history. The building was constructed in the 12th century by the Crusaders, but other nearby structures on the Temple Mount are up to 500 years older. Much of the ornamental work on display is breathtaking in its opulence and perfection.
Open: daily except Friday, 8:00 A.M.–4:00 P.M.
Buses: 1, 38

ISLAMIC ART MUSEUM
2 HaPalma Street
The beautiful pink-stoned building houses collections of ceramics, tapestry, clothing, metalwork, jewellery and calligraphy from Egypt, Syria, Turkey, Iraq, Iran and India, spanning the period from the 7th century till the present time.
Open: Sunday to Thursday 10:00 A.M.–1:00 P.M. and 3:30/6:00 P.M.; Saturday 10:00 A.M.–1:00 P.M.
Bus: 15

ISRAEL MUSEUM
Ruppin Street
The Israel Museum is the largest and most important museum in the country. Even if viewed superficially, it requires at least

Sculpture outside the main entrance to the Israel Museum

half a day. It incorporates, *inter alia*, the **Bezalel National Museum of Art**, the **Bronfman Biblical and Archaeological Museum**, the **Billy Rose Sculpture Garden**, the **Ruth Youth Wing** and the **Shrine of the Book**. The latter houses the Dead Sea Scrolls as well as other valuable biblical manuscripts. The museum offers something for all tastes: sculptures by Rodin, Henry Moore and Picasso, ancient coins, artefacts and sculptures; Jewish heritage exhibits representing most of the countries of Jewish dispersion; ethnic arts from all over the world; Jewish ethnography; fine arts; art for and by school children; period exhibits; posters; photography; films ...

A Henry Moore work displayed in the Billy Rose Garden of sculptures at the Israel Museum

and a cafeteria.
Open: Sunday, Monday, Wednesday, Thursday 10:00 A.M.–5:00 P.M.; Friday and Saturday 10:00 A.M.–2:00 P.M..
Tuesday: Museum 4:00/10:00 P.M., Shrine of the Book and Billy Rose Sculpture Garden 10:00 A.M.–10:00 P.M.; Tickets for Saturday must be purchased in advance at the museum or at Klaim Ticket Agency, 16 Shamai Street.
Buses: 9, 17, 24

◆◆
ITALIAN JEWISH MUSEUM
27 Hillel Street
In 1952, the synagogue of Conegliano Veneto, 35 miles (56 km) from Venice, was dismantled and brought to Jerusalem. Built in 1701, it was lovingly reassembled in the heart of the Holy City, where it continues to serve as a place of worship for the city's Italian Jewish community. The museum contains many exquisitely crafted ceremonial items preserved from other Italian synagogues. Some of these items are first-class examples of 15th- and 16th-century workmanship. Right outside the museum is an urban pocket park with drinking fountain. Unlike other pocket parks in the city, this one has more stone and less greenery.
Open: Sunday, Tuesday 10:00 A.M.–1:00 P.M.; Wednesday 4:00/7:00 P.M.. Other days by appointment
Buses: 4, 7, 8, 9, 14, 31, 32

◆
JEWISH ART MUSEUM
55 HaRav Zalman Sorotzkin Street
This is a private collection amassed by Rabbi Shlomo Pappenheim, who was eager to preserve artefacts of vanishing Jewish communities.
Open: by appointment
Bus: 3

 JEWISH MICROGRAPHICAL MUSEUM
43 HaNevi'im Street (in the Yad Sarah Building)
The museum, also known as the Avraham Haba Museum, is an astonishing collection of sacred Jewish texts and biographies of famous Jewish leaders which have been committed to parchment and paper in the minutest of script and decorative portraiture.
Open: Sunday to Thursday 9:00 A.M.–5:00 P.M.

 KOOK MUSEUM
9 HaRav Kook Street (off Zion Square)
The home of the country's first Chief Rabbi Abraham Yitzhak Hacohen Kook, the house contains a permanent exhibition devoted to his life and works. A pedagogical centre, located on the premises, fosters his teachings.

Montefiore's Windmill, a conspicuous landmark on the Jerusalem skyline

Open: Sunday to Thursday 9:00 A.M.–2:00 P.M.
Buses: 1, 5, 6, 11, 15

 MONTEFIORE'S WINDMILL
at the entrance to Yemin Moshe neighbourhood
Built by Sir Moses Montefiore to provide a source of livelihood for the first Jewish residents to build their homes outside the walls of the Old City, the Windmill has been converted into a museum depicting the history of the era in which it was built in the second half of the 19th century. It is now a landmark and the plaza surrounding the museum offers quite magnificent panoramic views.
Open: Sunday to Thursday 8:30 A.M.–4:30 P.M.; Friday 9:00 A.M.–1:00 P.M.
Buses: 5, 6, 7, 8, 14, 15, 21

NATURAL HISTORY MUSEUM
6 Mohiliver Street, German Colony
Established primarily as an educational resource for schoolchildren, the museum also has much to interest adults.
Open: Sunday to Thursday 9:00 A.M.–1:00 P.M.; Wednesday 4:00/6:00 P.M.
Buses: 4, 14, 18

OLD YISHUV COURT MUSEUM
6 Or Hahayim Street, Jewish Quarter, Old City
This was the private home of the Weingarten family up to 1948, when the Jewish Quarter of the Old City was conquered by the Jordanians. Rivka Weingarten, one of the daughters in the family, searched out everything that characterised the Jewish Quarter from 1880 to 1948. She incorporated everything she found into her former home, which she converted into a museum.
Open: Sunday to Thursday 9:00 A.M.–4:00 P.M.
Buses: 1, 38

OPEN EYE SCIENCE CENTRE
Giv'at Ram Campus, Hebrew University
The hands-on exhibits enable visitors to participate in scientific experiments and to have them explained on a step-by-step basis by staff members. This is a particularly good place to come with children.
Open: Sunday to Friday 9.00 A.M.–1:00 P.M.; Tuesday to 6:00 P.M.; Saturday 10:00 A.M.–3:00 P.M.
Buses: 9, 24

PALESTINIAN ARAB FOLKLORE CENTRE
Ibn Haldoun Street, East Jerusalem
Much of Palestinian folklore is contained in stitchery. Certain types of embroidery immediately designate the origin of the embroidery. These and other features of Palestinian life can be seen at the centre.
Open: by appointment
Buses: 23, 27

PALOMBO MUSEUM
Mount Zion
The works of Jerusalem sculptor David Palombo, creator of the distinctive gates at the Knesset and the Yad Vashem Museum, who met his death in a motor cycle accident on Mount Zion in 1967 are on display here.
Open: by appointment
Buses: 1, 3, 20, 38

PAPAL BIBLE MUSEUM
Emile Botta Street
Archaeological museum and comprehensive, multi-lingual library housed in one of the most magnificent buildings in Jerusalem.
Open: Monday to Thursday 9:00 A.M.–noon
Buses: 5, 6, 15, 18, 21

ROCKEFELLER MUSEUM
Sultan Suleiman Street, East Jerusalem
Administered by the Israel Museum, the Rockefeller Museum was previously known as The Palestine Museum of Archaeology. Built around a

The inner courtyard of the Rockefeller Museum

courtyard, it has several galleries, each of which focuses on a different period of ancient history.
Open: Sunday to Thursday 10:00 A.M.–5:00 P.M.; Saturday until 2:00 P.M.
Buses: *23, 27*

◆◆ SCHOCKEN INSTITUTE OF JEWISH RESEARCH
6 Balfour Street
Jewish illuminated manuscripts from 13th century onwards.
Open: Sunday to Thursday 9:00 A.M.–1:00 P.M.
Buses: 9, 17, 22, 31, 32

◆ SECOND TEMPLE MODEL
next to Holyland Hotel, Bayit Vegan
Impressive scale model of

Second Temple, the original of which was destroyed in AD70.
Open: daily 8:00 A.M.–5:00 P.M.
Buses: 21, 21a

◆ SIEBENBERG HOUSE
7 Hagitit Street, Jewish Quarter, Old City
When Theo and Miriam Siebenberg moved into this house in the late 1960s, they got caught up in the excavation fever around them. They decided to dig in the basement area of their own house and came up with many interesting finds.
Open: 9:00 A.M.–5:00 P.M. Guided tours and slide shows at noon.
Buses: 1, 38

MUSEUMS

SKIRBALL MUSEUM
*Hebrew Union College, 13
David haMelekh (King David)
Street*
A museum of continuous history.
The focus is primarily on
archaeological excavations
carried out by the Hebrew Union
College's Nelson Glueck School
of Biblical Archaeology. The
exhibits are augmented by
models and photographs of the
sites in which they were found.
Open: Sunday to Thursday
10:00A.M.–4:00P.M.; Friday,
Saturday until 2P.M.
Buses: 5, 6, 15, 18, 21

TAXATION MUSEUM
32 Agron Street
Situated in a wing of the Ministry
of Commerce and Industry, the
Museum reflects the history of
taxation from the period of the
Ottoman Empire.
Open: Sunday, Tuesday,
Thursday 1:00P.M.–4:00P.M.
Buses: 5, 6, 15, 18, 21

TICHO HOUSE
7 Harav Kook Street
Well over 100 years old, the
house, set in spacious garden
surrounds, was inhabited by a
succession of owners, the last of
whom was the noted painter
Anna Ticho, who bequeathed it
to the people of Jerusalem. It is
now a museum and cultural
centre.
There is also a dairy restaurant
on the premises.
Open: Sunday to Thursday
10:A.M.–5:00P.M.; Tuesday until
10:00P.M.; Friday until 2:00P.M.
Buses: 1, 3, 5, 6, 11, 15

TOURJEMAN POST MUSEUM
*corner of Damascus Road and
Hayil Hahandasa Street*
Badly damaged during the 1948
war, this impressive example of
Arab architecture for 19 years
was the Israeli military border
post adjacent to the
Mandelbaum Gate, which
served as the border crossing
between Israel and Jordan.
Following the reunification of the
city, the building was partly
restored and turned into a
museum dedicated to the future
aversion of any war which would
again divide the city.
Open: Sunday to Friday
9:00 A.M.–4:00 P.M.; Tuesday until
6:00 P.M., Friday until 1:00 P.M.
Buses: 1, 3, 11, 27

TOWER OF DAVID MUSEUM
Jaffa Gate, Old City
This is an absolutely wonderful
museum detailing 3,000 years of
history with the help of models,
diorama, holograms, maps and
diagrams. Clear, concise text
alongside each exhibit helps to
give the visitor a broad
understanding of the history of
Jerusalem.
Open: at time of writing museum
closed until further notice.
Buses: 1, 13, 19, 20, 23, 38

WOHL HERODIAN MUSEUM
*Hurvah Square, Jewish Quarter,
Old City*
Located below ground level,
beneath the premises of a
religious seminary, the museum
offers an even better
perspective than the Burnt
House of Kathros of the living

quarters of the Jewish nobility during the Herodian period. Some of the original mosaic floor remains, as do the foundations, the room divisions and the ritual baths. The mansions have been refurnished with household items excavated from the ruins and has been painstakingly restored.

Open: Sunday to Thursday 9:00 A.M.–5:00 P.M.; Friday 9:00 A.M.–1:00 P.M.
Buses: 1, 38

◆◆
WOLFSON MUSEUM

58 HaMalekh George (King George) Street
Located in the headquarters of the Chief Rabbinate is a collection of extremely interesting Jewish ceremonial art.

Open: Sunday to Thursday 9:00 A.M.–1:00 P.M.; Friday until noon
Buses: 4, 7, 8, 9, 14, 17, 19, 22, 31, 32

◆◆◆
YAD VASHEM

Har HaZikkaron 'Mount of Remembrance', behind Mount Herzl
A grim reminder of man's capacity for inhumanity, this museum dedicated to the memories of the martyrs of the Nazi Holocaust is not for the faint-hearted. Mostly a photographic exhibition of huge enlargements of snapshots, official German records and evidence gathered from every possible source, the museum is the most extensive and important of its kind in the world. There are over 50 million documents in Yad Vashem's central archives. An art museum

contains the works of ghetto and concentration camp artists. The Valley of Destroyed Communities, similar in concept to the memorial on the site of the Treblinka death camp in Poland, contains engravings on stone of the names of 5,000 of those communities in 22 countries. A separate memorial to the one and a half million Jewish children who perished in the Holocaust is based on light and mirrors. One flickering candle is reflected thousands of times while recorded voices recite the names of the dead children. A memorial chapel with the names of all the death camps has six million stone chips in the floor—one for each of the six million Jews killed in the Holocaust. In the midst of all this devastation is an arbour of hope—the avenue of the Righteous Gentiles bordered by trees, each of which is planted in the name of a non-Jew who risked death to save Jewish lives. Where possible, the people whose names and heroism are enshrined in perpetuity have been brought to Israel to plant the saplings from which the trees have grown. Yad Vashem also serves as an international centre for Holocaust studies and conducts many seminars throughout the year. Visitors who cannot tear themselves away without inspecting the whole complex should count on spending a whole day. There is a cafeteria on the grounds.

Open: Sunday to Thursday 9:00 A.M.–4:45 P.M.; Friday until 12:45 P.M.
Buses: 99. Also 17, 18, 20, 21, 23, 27 to Mount Herzl, then walk.

Excursions

BETHLEHEM

Lying about six miles (10km) from Jerusalem, Bethlehem makes an easy, short excursion. There are frequent bus services to Bethlehem from near the Damascus and Jaffa Gates, as well as from the main bus station. Bethlehem (Beit Lahm), birthplace of Jesus and ancestral home of King David, is in Israeli-occupied Palestine and is a lively town, as well as a centre of pilgrimage for millions of people around the world. Tourism has become a major source of income for many of the residents, most of whom are Christian Arabs, and there are colourful markets and bazaars. Most visitors come to Bethlehem to see the **Church of the Nativity**, off Manger Square. In AD326, the Emperor Constantine had a basilica built over a grotto here, on the outskirts of Bethlehem village, marking the site where Jesus was believed to have been born. About 200 years later, the basilica was demolished and, in its place, the Church of the Nativity was built. This is now one of the few buildings to survive, virtually intact, from the early Christian era. Justinian had the present structure built, intending it to be the most impressive in Jerusalem—but don't expect lavish decoration. The interior is sombre, with brown limestone pillars and an oak roof. The Grotto of the Nativity is reached from either side of the Greek Orthodox High Altar (the Church is shared by the Greek Orthodox, Latins and Armenians). Lit by 53 lamps, this 40ft (12m) long room may once have been used as a cattle shelter. Beneath the altar is a silver star, with the inscription *Hic de Virgine Maria Jesus Christus natus est* (Here Jesus Christ was born of the Virgin Mary). Squabbles over ownership of the grotto centred around the star which Roman Catholics first placed here, to the chagrin of the Greek Orthodox. The ensuing territorial and political wrangles were a part of the escalating tensions which led to the Crimean War.

Not far from the Church is the **Grotto of the Milk**. According to tradition, a drop of milk fell from Mary's breast to the ground and turned the rock white. The present buildings date from 1872, but fragments survive of earlier churches, and the Franciscans have owned the grotto since about 1350.

Beit Sahur (Village of the Shepherds), is about half a mile (1km) east of Bethlehem; here, the Field of Ruth is reputedly where Boaz saw and fell in love with Ruth, as told in the Old Testament.

The Tomb of Rachel, whose present domed building dates from the 18th to 19th centuries, is one and a quarter miles (2km) north of Bethlehem.

The Herodion, a fortress built by Herod the Great in the hollowed-out mountain is six miles (10km) southeast of Bethlehem; he is said to be buried here, but his tomb has yet to be discovered.

See **Tours and Excursions** in the **Directory** for places to visit further afield from Jerusalem.

PEACE AND QUIET

Wildlife and Countryside
in and around Jerusalem
by Paul Sterry

Most first-time visitors to Israel
are amazed by the variety of
habitats and landscapes to be
found within the boundaries of
this comparatively small country.
With its geographical position in
the Middle East, few are
surprised at the country's
deserts; but the contrasts of the
lush, tropical vegetation of En
Gedi, the snow-capped peak of
Mount Hermon, the
extraordinary scenery of the
Dead Sea and the coral reefs of
Eilat on the Red Sea are truly
unexpected. Not surprisingly,
this diversity is reflected in the
wealth of Israel's wildlife and
this, together with its position on
a major bird migration route,
make it an unparalleled

destination for naturalists,
especially in spring.
Man's settlement of the land has
had a marked effect upon the
wildlife of Israel. Jackals and
other scavenging animals have
suffered persecution, but his
influence has not been to the
detriment of all species.
Irrigation and cultivation of arid
areas and the development of
kibbutz settlements have
assisted many birds.
In common with arid areas
throughout the world, the
wetland areas have suffered
badly. Drainage has destroyed
many sites but, fortunately,
reserves have saved remnants of
the best areas. As an
unexpected bonus, however,
fish pond schemes have
recreated regimented areas of

*Dry wadis hold more animal life
than the surrounding desert*

PEACE AND QUIET

A Red Sea clownfish sheltering in an anemone: one of the countless colourful species found at Eilat

marsh and lake, which have inadvertently served to replace the lost wetlands.

Jerusalem itself occupies a fairly central position in the country and is within easy driving distance of the Negev Desert, the Mediterranean coast and En Gedi. Even outstanding sites like Eilat, Lake Tiberias, the Hula Nature Reserve and the Golan Heights can be reached in a day and offer alternatives to sightseeing tours within the city. If you lack your own transportation, there is still plenty to see in Jerusalem and the countryside immediately surrounding it. Cicadas and other insects sing incessantly from trees and bushes, and many fall prey to migrant birds such as masked shrikes and blackcaps and resident Sardinian warblers. Geckos scurry over walls and buildings, and unwary

individuals fall victim, in undisturbed areas, to lesser kestrels and blue rock thrushes.

Eilat

Eilat is a popular coastal destination for thousands of tourists each year. It also has a worldwide reputation among ornithologists as being one of the best places in Europe to observe migrating birds, and thousands of enthusiasts visit the area specifically to enjoy this spectacle. By way of contrast, however, the deep blue waters of the Red Sea, which bathe the shores of Eilat, harbour fantastic coral reefs and offer relaxation during the heat of the day.

Eilat's attraction to migrant birds is partly due to its geographical position and partly to the variety of habitats which make up the region. Agricultural land, wadis, shady groves of date palms, beaches and salt pans offer an opportunity to feed, drink and rest for birds heading north into Europe and Asia, having crossed the African deserts from their wintering grounds. Countless hundreds of thousands of birds of prey alone pass through each year, and almost any migrant songbird on the European list is likely to turn up.

Spring migration starts in early March and extends into May and, as with other migration spots, early mornings are the best time of day to birdwatch. This is especially true where birds of prey and storks are concerned, since they use daytime thermals to assist their passage and rise to considerable heights by midday. Steppe eagles, black kites, lesser spotted eagles, Levant sparrowhawks, pallid harriers, honey buzzards and ospreys pass through regularly, with many other species occurring less frequently. Mixed flocks of raptors are often seen alongside flocks of white storks and black storks. The same phenomenon can be observed during autumn migration.

Open, grassy fields such as the local soccer field are a favourite haunt of Cretzschmar's buntings and wheatears, and up to 10 species of the latter may be recorded in a two-week period. Bushes, plantations and the kibbutz fields, on the other hand, harbour masked shrikes, collared flycatchers, numerous species of warblers and bee-eaters.

Waders and water birds also pass through Eilat in considerable numbers. Some may stop off on the coast, but most favour the saltpans and sewage works. Spotted, little and Baillon's crakes are found on surprisingly small areas of water, while spur-winged plovers, wood sandpipers, marsh sandpipers and pratincoles prefer the shores of larger pools. Egrets and herons can also be found wading in the water, while several species of tern grace the air above.

Eilat lies at the head of the Red Sea, and the offshore waters harbour an amazing richness of marine life. The coral reef can be explored by boat or with the aid of a snorkel, and shoals of fish such as black spotted grunts, anemones with attendant clownfish, and colourful starfish, as well as the corals themselves can easily be seen.

Ma'agan Mikhael

Ma'agan Mikhael is an area of fish ponds and marsh in northern Israel which lies close to the Mediterranean coast between Hadera and Haifa. Among wildlife enthusiasts, it is renowned for the numbers and variety of water birds that it attracts, and is especially productive during spring and autumn migration. Although part of Ma'agan Mikhael has restricted access during the breeding season, there is plenty to see in accessible areas at any time and waders, herons, egrets, pelicans and flamingos provide a bonanza for the birdwatchers. Around the banks of the ponds, redshanks, marsh sandpipers, wood sandpipers, spur-winged plovers and black-winged stilts wade elegantly in the water. Small species of wader such as common sandpiper, greater sandplovers and Temminck's stints are often abundant and feed actively right at the water's edge.

Thanks to their long legs, greater flamingos can wade deep in the water, filtering tiny aquatic organisms from the water with their strangely shaped bills. White-winged black terns and whiskered terns hawk for flies over the water, while slender-billed gulls pick small fish and crustaceans from the surface. Larger fish fall victim to little egrets, night herons, glossy ibises, white pelicans, white storks, pied kingfishers and Smyrna kingfishers.

Along the beach, several species of tern may be found roosting, and turnstones and Kentish plovers chase after small insects and crustaceans.

Due to evaporation, the Dead Sea is extremely saline

En Gedi and the Dead Sea

The Dead Sea and surrounding land comprise some of the most inhospitable terrain on Earth. At 1,300 feet (400m) *below* sea level, the evaporating waters are highly saline and, although an impressive sight with their pillars of salt, support little in the way of wildlife. However, although the scrub and desert bordering the Dead Sea may also appear arid and lifeless, a little exploration will reveal a range of interesting birds and mammals. Wadis, or dry river beds, are particularly rewarding for the naturalist, and at En Gedi a lush, tropical oasis with pools and waterfalls can be found all year round.

Although arid and dry for most of the year, wadis often have a colourful carpet of flowers in spring, especially if the previous

winter's rains have been good. Insects are drawn to these areas and lizards scurry over the stony ground. Birds such as desert lark, Tristram's grackle, white-crowned black wheatear, scrub warbler, Arabian babbler and blackstart may be found and, early in the morning, migrant warblers, chats and wheatears rest and feed in the bushes. Rocky outcrops and broken hillsides are the haunt of Nubian ibexes. These sure-footed ancestors of the goat possess long, curved horns when full grown, and can scramble over the most difficult and broken terrain. Sand partridges, trumpeter finches, fan-tailed ravens and brown-necked ravens also favour this habitat, as do migrant and resident birds of prey. Cliff-top vantage points, and in particular the hill fort at

Masada, offer the best opportunities of seeing raptors such as buzzards, honey buzzards, lesser spotted eagles, steppe eagles and griffon vultures; and lammergeiers sometimes float by at eye level. The nature reserve at En Gedi, open from 9:00 A.M., offers the best opportunities along the shores of the Dead Sea for seeing the birds of the area, amid vegetation which remains green throughout the year. Unusual birds such as Hume's tawny owl are often located by visitors, and commoner species, such as Palestine sunbird and yellow-vented bulbul, are often more trustful than elsewhere. En Gedi is also the haunt of a most unusual mammal – the rock hyrax. Despite its superficial similarity to a guinea pig, its closest living relative is thought to be the elephant.

A desert Ibex: perfectly at home in the stony desert

The Negev Desert

The Negev Desert occupies the southern half of Israel between the Arava valley in the east and the Egyptian border in the west. Viewed by Israel's pioneer colonists as frontier country, the Negev has long been a source of friction between Israel and its neighbours as witnessed by the continued military presence in the area. Fortunately, the desert creatures do not recognise boundaries and disputes, and many still thrive in the hostile terrain. While for some the Negev may be barren and featureless, most people find a strange and unique fascination in this desert region, and wonder at the occasional wealth of spring flowers and at the hardy nature of its animal inhabitants.

After a winter of heavy rains, spring sees a miraculous transformation of the Negev from a dusty plain into a carpet of colourful flowers. The wadis, or river valleys, that normally run dry for most of the year, hold on to moisture after the rains have ceased and allow particularly luxuriant and extended growth. Flowers of thistles, crocuses, daisies, anemones and sages, whose seeds or underground tubers and bulbs have remained dormant through the drought, appear almost overnight, and you might be forgiven for comparing the flora with that of a meadow.

These wadis, in spring, are also good sites to search for some of the more unusual animals of the desert. Shiny, black beetles plod deliberately over the sand, and lizards scurry for the cover of rock crevices. Although shy, Dorca's gazelles are sometimes seen, and at dusk there is always a chance of seeing one of the desert's small rodents, or even a jackal.

Birdlife is also rich in the desert,

PEACE AND QUIET

*This really is a desert! Flowers
in profusion after winter rains*

and often congregates close to
wadis. Mourning and desert
wheatears, spectacled warblers,
pin-tailed and black-bellied
sandgrouse are all widespread,
but the prize of the Negev is
undoubtedly the Houbara
bustard. Now one of the world's
most endangered species, these
large birds can still be found by
patient searching, although their
wary nature and keen senses
mean that distant views are
typical. Away from the wadis,
desert larks, hoopoe larks, stone
curlews and cream-coloured
coursers seem content with the
driest conditions, relying on
insects and seeds to provide
enough water for their needs.

The Golan Heights and Mount Hermon

Lying in the far northeast of the
country, close to the Syrian
border, these two areas offer a
range of scenery and habitats
quite different from that found in

the south of Israel. The rolling,
cultivated fields, pools and
eroded cliffs and rock formations
of the Golan Heights, and the
wooded slopes and snow-
capped peak of Mount Hermon
are quite an unexpected contrast
to deserts and coast. Since the
Six Days War, the whole area
has been militarily sensitive, and
visitors should exercise a
degree of caution and common
sense about where they wander
and when they use binoculars
and cameras.

Many parts of the Golan Heights
have been settled and cultivated
in recent years. Tilled soils, as
well as undisturbed land, attract
Spanish sparrows, crested larks,
short-toed larks and Calandra
larks, which search the ground
for seeds and insects such as
grasshoppers, crickets and
beetles. Calandra larks may be
confused at first glance with the
much rarer bimaculated lark,
which breeds in small numbers
on the slopes of Mount Hermon.
European wheatears and
isabelline wheatears also favour

this habitat in spring and summer while, in winter, large flocks of finches and buntings pass through the region. Some remain here through the winter into spring, and flocks sometimes comprise an interesting range of species. Birds of prey pass through the Golan Heights on spring and autumn migration, often in considerable numbers; honey buzzards and black kites may be seen at the same time as resident griffon vultures.

At over 7,200 feet (2,200m), Mount Hermon is Israel's highest mountain, with such a reliable supply of snow that a ski resort is located here. Rock sparrow, Cretzschmar's bunting, rock nuthatch, black redstart and black-eared wheatear prefer areas of broken, stony ground, while wooded areas hold sombre tit and Tristram's serin. At the highest levels, alpine choughs cavort aerobatically, and the delightful crimson-winged finch may be found.

Hula Nature Reserve

Nestling between hills and mountains in the northeast of Israel, the Hula valley was once a vast area of lake and swamp, which attracted huge numbers of migrant birds. Sadly, the last 30 years have seen drainage and reclamation affect most of the wetland, but, fortunately, over 700 acres (280 hectares) are now a nature reserve and thoughtfully sited hides and trails give superb views over the remaining marshland.

One of the more interesting features of the vegetation is the presence of papyrus swamps,

recorded in the Middle East since biblical times, but more at home in truly tropical regions. Reedbeds and large areas of water-lily add to the variety; and, in drier areas, tamarisk bushes provide cover for small birds such as Dead Sea sparrows, and patches of dense vegetation serve as winter roosts for marsh and hen harriers. The waters teem with fish and amphibians, which, in turn, feed otters and huge numbers of water birds.

In spring and autumn, flocks of white pelicans drop into Hula on their way to and from wintering grounds in Africa and breeding lakes in Europe and Asia. Even when feeding, the flocks remain loosely together, which is in marked contrast to grey, purple, night and squacco herons, which have more solitary habits. Little bitterns creep quietly through the reeds, their small size allowing them to clamber through vegetation without bending it, while little and great egrets wade deeply in the water.

Clamorous reed warblers and moustached warblers sing from the tops of the reeds, announcing their presence within a territory. Many of the other permanent and temporary residents of the Hula marshes are less obtrusive, however, and water rails and crakes require luck and patience to be seen.

Of particular interest among the wildfowl are the marbled teals which breed on Hula; despite the camouflage that their dappled plumage affords them, they are sometimes seen dabbling close to the cover of vegetation.

PEACE AND QUIET

Lake Tiberias

Lake Tiberias, also known as the Sea of Galilee, lies in the northeast of Israel and is nearly 700 feet (200m) below sea level. The deep blue waters of the lake, which harbour a healthy population of fish, are framed by a backdrop of mountains and margins lush with vegetation. Despite the fact that the waters are rich in aquatic life, the variety of birds found on Lake Tiberias is small, especially when compared to the nearby Hula reserve, but the fauna and flora

Large numbers of water birds, such as this glossy ibis, pass through Israel on migration

that can be found in the surrounding wadis and fish ponds make up for this.

In spring, bushes and trees bordering Lake Tiberias should be searched for Syrian woodpeckers and migrants such as flycatchers, blackcaps, Ruppell's warblers and Orphean warblers. A few herons and egrets feed along the shore, while the occasional slender-billed gull and pied kingfisher

are seen over the water. Ducks and grebes winter on the lake, but for a greater variety of birdlife, the fish ponds at Bet She'an, to the south of the lake, should be visited. Here, an abundance of waders, ibises, herons, egrets, storks and ospreys can be seen with crakes, rails and warblers frequenting patches of marshland vegetation.

Several interesting wadis can be found to the north and west of Lake Tiberias. Many are worth visiting for their scenic beauty alone, because centuries of winter rains have carved deep gorges and dramatic cliffs into the parched land. The native wildlife has often benefited from this erosion, and the rock faces now serve as nesting sites for birds such as blue rock thrush, eagle owl, long-legged buzzard, griffon vulture, Egyptian vulture and little swift.

In spring, the valley floors of many wadis, such as Wadi Kziv, are carpeted with colourful flowers, which attract insects as well as black francolins and long-billed pipits. Wadi Tabor has permanent water, and the lush vegetation harbours many migrants during spring and autumn, as well as Syrian woodpeckers and yellow-vented bulbuls. Geckos and other lizards are often abundant on broken, rocky slopes and, with luck, some of Israel's desert mammals may also be seen. Rocky hyraxes stare down from rocky vantage points, and gazelles disappear into the heat haze while, at dusk, desert rodents and genets may be fleetingly glimpsed.

FOOD AND DRINK

Jerusalem's population comes from more than a hundred ethnic backgrounds. This diversity is reflected in the ever-growing variety of restaurants and fast-food establishments. For a long time, the latter were dominated by the cuisines of the Middle East, but in recent years there has been a surge of pizza parlours, sandwich bars and stores specialising in baked goods straight out of the oven. Standards vary, but the lack of quality is compensated for by quantity. Portions are seldom skimpy. When dining in a restaurant you will find that your plate is well covered.

The less expensive restaurants usually include two side dishes—french fries and salad—with the main courses, without extra charge; but in more expensive restaurants, where the side dishes are

Fresh fruits on display in a fruit juice bar

often served on separate plates, they are charged for separately.

If you have had no previous experience with Jewish or Muslim dietary laws, you may be frustrated by the difficulties in trying to get a ham sandwich or a plate of bacon and eggs. Pork is forbidden to both Jews and Muslims, although irreligious members of both faiths tend to ignore this stricture.

Eating establishments which proclaim themselves to be kosher—fit for Jewish consumption—do not serve meat and dairy foods together, nor do they serve the meat of animals which do not chew the cud and have fully cloven hooves, the meat of birds of prey, fish which do not have fins and scales, amphibians and reptiles. Most of the laws pertaining to the creatures which Jews may or may not consume are to be found in the biblical books of *Deuteronomy* and *Leviticus*. There is also a

FOOD AND DRINK

biblical injunction against cooking a kid in its mother's milk, from which derives the total separation of meat and dairy dishes. Strictly observant Jews wait six hours after consuming meat to partake of dairy foods; and an hour after eating dairy foods to partake of meat. If they have been eating hard, yellow cheese, which takes longer to digest, then they wait six hours. When dining in a kosher restaurant with a meat menu, you will not be able to have milk or cream in your tea or coffee; but in some places, you will be offered a non-dairy creamer. Israeli chefs have done marvels in substituting vegetable derivatives for milk and cream in order to serve kosher beef Strogonoff, creamed mushrooms to be served with meat, vegetarian ice creams and puddings, and a host of other delicacies.

Vegetarian

Jerusalem's dairy restaurants will delight vegetarians. They don't have to worry that their crockery or cutlery may have been in contact with meat products; and unless they happen to abstain from fish and eggs, their menu choices are not as limited as they are in most restaurants elsewhere in the world. Vegans too, will find it much easier to select their meals in Jerusalem than in most other capitals of the world.

Middle Eastern

Bland foods are not for the Middle Eastern palate. Most Middle Eastern foods are spicy, and many are also oily. A typical

Middle Eastern meal begins with a stack of fresh *pitas*, the flat Arab bread envelope, and anything from five to 15 small plates of savoury dips such as eggplant, *houmous* (ground chickpeas) and *tahina* (sesame paste), pickled turnips, radishes and cucumbers, relishes and *felafel* (deep fried chickpea balls), *ful* (a slow-cooked bean hash) and *kube* (fried burghul dumplings with ground beef or lamb, onions and spices). Occasionally, there may be *yapra*, a piquant dish of spicy rice and ground meat rolled in vine leaves. This is a meal in itself, but for diners with large appetites, there are pungent soups with a variety of dumplings, and charcoal-grilled skewered meats which include such delicacies as bulls' testicles.

Standards of hygiene in Middle

Pita *bread,* felafel, *various sauces and salads – a typical meal*

Eastern restaurants in West Jerusalem are generally higher than those in East Jerusalem, as are the prices. A string of restaurants serving Middle Eastern specialities can be found in Agrippas Street in West Jerusalem. Of these, the one with the highest reputation is **Sima's**, almost on the edge of the Mahane Yeduha market. It is just slightly more expensive than its competitors.

The filled *pita* is *the* staple for eat-in-the-street Israelis. In many establishments, behind-the-counter staff will fill it with *felafel* or *shwarma* (thin slices of broiled turkey or lamb cut from a rotating vertical spit), char-broiled poultry giblets, kebabs (spiced ground meat) or cubes of beef or lamb, leaving the customer to choose from a sauce, salad and other extras. There is a set price regardless of how much or how little you may stuff into your own *pita.* You have to be careful when eating it, because the bottom is inclined to burst.

Sandwiches

It is extremely rare to find a regular sliced bread sandwich in Israel, although the signboard on the premises may designate the establishment as a sandwich shop. Sandwiches in Israel are of the *pita* variety, or rolls. More recently, the *baguette* fad has caught on, and a *baguette* filled with creamy cheeses, avocado salad, tuna or anything else is offered widely.

European

For the most part, the European cuisines available in Jerusalem originate from Central Europe and the Baltic States. In the fast-food range, the most popular item is the Bulgarian *boureka,* a triangle of flaky pastry filled with cheese, spinach or potato. Another favourite European dish is the *blintz,* which is basically a rolled *crêpe* filled with cream cheese in its sweet version and mushrooms in its savoury version. Some restaurants also serve meat *blintzes,* the filling for which is made from ground beef or from liver pâté. If you order a *shnitzel* in any Israeli restaurant, don't expect the Viennese variety unless the menu specifies veal. Poultry is comparatively cheap in Israel, and *shnitzel* is almost always made from turkey or chicken breasts.

FOOD AND DRINK

American

Whether or not the hamburger is strictly an American invention remains debatable, but American-style hamburger joints are beginning to spring up in Jerusalem, and are fairly successful because they offer filling and affordable meals which are neither surprisingly good nor disappointingly bad. There are also American-style delis.

Asian

A number of Chinese restaurants, both kosher and non-kosher, have opened in the last 10 years or so, although their culinary offerings are not definitively Chinese, a factor which can be attributed to the fact that most of the cooks are not Chinese, but come from different

A street café in Ben Yehuda Street

parts of Asia. It is also possible to get Vietnamese and Korean food in Jerusalem.

The brief selection of Jerusalem restaurants which follows gives some indication of the city's broad culinary canvas. When you are actually in Jerusalem you will be able to get a more comprehensive picture through publications available at the front desks of hotels and at the Ministry of Tourism. All these publications are free of charge. They include *Your Jerusalem*, *This Week in Jerusalem*, *Hello Israel*, and *Jerusalem Menus*. With the exception of hotel restaurants, most restaurants in West Jerusalem and a few in East Jerusalem are closed on Friday nights and all day Saturday. Those which remain open will be listed first in *Jerusalem Menus*.

Non-Kosher Restaurants

American Colony Hotel, Nablus Road, East Jerusalem (tel: 285 171). Attractive for its ambience as well as its cuisine. A favourite haunt of diplomats and foreign journalists. Seven-course candlelit dinner on Friday night; sumptuous buffet lunch on Saturday. Continental and Middle Eastern medley.

Cannibal Restaurant and Pub, 21 Khutzot HaYotzer (Arts and Crafts Lane) (tel: 272 276). Steaks are the speciality of the house, and are washed down with draught beer drawn from the barrel, which is a rather rare treat in Israel. Indoor and outdoor dining. Live music.

Chez Pe'er, corner of Ben Shetah and Hasoreg Streets (tel: 231 793 or 233 424 evenings). Elegant, high-priced seafood restaurant with a French flavour.

Chez Simon, 15 Shammay Street (tel: 225 602). As the name suggests, the cuisine is French. What is more important is that it enjoys an international reputation. Non-Jerusalemites who eat here once return with each succeeding visit. Price-wise, the restaurant, with its fully stocked bar, is for patrons in the upper income bracket. It is well worth the high cost and one can rarely find a table by just walking in off the street.

Primavera, 1 Washington Street (corner of King David Street) (tel: 435 778). Delightful Italian garden restaurant specialising in North Italian cuisine. All the pasta is made on the premises. Slightly on the expensive side, but definitely worth a visit.

Pie House, YMCA, 26 King David Street (tel: 227 111). Delicious nouvelle cuisine meat, fish and vegetarian meals with absolutely mouth-watering last courses. All food freshly prepared and served in the supreme elegance of a superbly designed building, which for more than a century has been a Jerusalem landmark. You can drop in as early as 7:00 A.M. or as late as midnight. Good value.

Mandarin, 2 Shlomzion Hamalka Street (tel: 222 890). The restaurant which pioneered Chinese food in Israel. Prices are reasonable and the service is good.

Me Va Me 34 Ben Yehuda Street (in the cellar of the Eilon Tower building) (tel: 242 214). A good variety of fish, meat and salad dishes. Attractive, casual environment. Open from 11:00 A.M. to 1:00 A.M. Reasonably priced.

Notre Dame, 8 Shivte Yisra'el Street (tel: 288 018). Situated in the magnificent Notre Dame Cathedral complex, the restaurant has the reputation of being one of the finest in Israel. The cuisine borders on the French. Prices are reasonable.

Drink

One of the greatest pleasures in Israel is the freshly squeezed citrus fruit juices. Vegetable juices, too, are to be found everywhere.

It's probably safer to stick to bottled water, always available, although tap water is safe to drink.

Very little alcohol is drunk in Israel generally, though there are some good local wines. Beers tend to be low alcohol but pleasant.

SHOPPING

Anyone who comes to Jerusalem looking for bargains is likely to be disappointed. Although Jerusalem is part of the Levant, its prices are not those of the bazaar. Electronic equipment is no cheaper than in Europe, and usually more expensive than in the US or Hong Kong. Shopping opportunities, compared to other world capitals, are somewhat sparse. Shopping malls are a relatively new phenomenon as far as Jerusalem is concerned, and, in general, are not overly successful. The Centre 1 Shopping Mall at the entrance to the city started off with a bang which could not be sustained. Shops are generally open from 8:30 A.M. to 7:00 P.M. Sunday to Thursday, and till 1:00 P.M. on Fridays. Some Jerusalem merchants are closed on Tuesday afternoons and others open on Saturday nights. Shops operating inside hotels frequently stay open till 10:00 P.M. Although shops and postal services in West Jerusalem are closed on Saturdays, those in Salah-al-Din Street and other parts of East Jerusalem are open when there are no strikes or curfews.

One of the *intifada* tactics is the placing of extreme limits on the hours in which East Jerusalem shops are open for business. The ploy has cost shopkeepers a small fortune in lost income, and some of them are actually quite glad when Israeli authorities occasionally force them to open their premises to the public. The *intifada* has also influenced the closure of Jewish-owned shops. With the drop in number of tourists, many shops dealing in wares which have more appeal to tourists than to locals, have found it unprofitable to stay open. It is also depressing to be open and have no-one come inside all day. Most of the shops in the Cardo, a commercial centre dating back to Roman times, were temporarily closed or changed ownership during the first 18 months of the INTIFADA. Now, with the slight resurgence in tourism, the shopkeepers are more optimistic—and some of the shops in and around the Cardo remain open all day. The Cardo is in the Jewish Quarter of the Old City.

Cameras and Optical Equipment

Jerusalem cannot compete with other developed capitals in terms of price, quantity and variety. None the less, there are ample choices for travellers who have forgotten to pack their own equipment. The best places to look in down-town Jerusalem are inside the King George Street/Jaffa Road/Ben Yehuda Mall triangle, as well as in Shamai and Hillel Streets, which run parallel to Ben Yehuda. Several of the small side streets off Ben Yehuda Street also stock this kind of merchandise.

Jewellery

Israel boasts some truly unique designs in both costume jewellery and in precious metals set with precious and semi-precious stones. Visitors who want something pretty and different, but don't want to pay too much, will find a large choice offered to them by street

vendors in the Ben Yehuda Mall and in the adjacent Zion Square. Many of the vendors are students or graduates of the Bezalel Academy of Design. For something in a higher price bracket, the international chain of quality jewellery stores, Sterns, operates in most 5-star hotels in Israel. Also worth a visit is Padani at 19 King David Street, near the King David Hotel. Ruth Matar, a world-renowned jewellery designer, produces a wide range of handmade jewellery at her studio/workshop in Yemin Moshe. Adipaz, the largest manufacturers and exporters of gold jewellery in the Middle East, sell to tourists at factory prices. They will transport visitors from their hotels to their factory showroom in the Talpiot Industrial Zone free of charge or obligation. Sigal, whose factory premises are in the Giv'at Sha'ul industrial zone, will also transport tourists free of charge or obligation. Full details of these manufacturers are available in tourist publications at hotels.

Jewellery is popular with visitors looking for something attractive and a bit different

Clothing and Fabrics

Given the fact that so many Jews abroad are involved in the garment trade, one would imagine that Israel would be *the* garment district of the world. Not so. Clothing in general is too highly priced in Israel, but one can find the occasional bargain. There are numerous clothing stores in down-town Jerusalem, the Bet haKerem Mall, the Centre 1 Mall and the Mall in the Talpiot Industrial Zone. For something in the way of ethnic design, the bazaars in the Old City are a must. If the beautifully embroidered Arab dresses hanging outside the stores catch your eye, you will probably be doubly fascinated when you go inside.

Most Arab storekeepers enjoy haggling over the price. **Tadmor Leather** at 16 King George Street and **Gingette** in the Laromme Hotel shopping arcade offer special reductions for tourists.

SHOPPING

Carpets

The **Maskit** store in Harav Kook Street has many one-of-a-kind carpets on display. The designs are usually modern. For something more traditional, take a look at the carpet stores in King David Street. Arab carpets and sheepskin rugs can be purchased in the Old City.

Shop around for carpets and ritual objects of every kind

Antiques

There are several antique shops in Jerusalem stocking crystals, pottery and silverware which settlers from Europe a century ago brought with them. Some antique shops also have samples of the fine hand embroidery which 50 years ago and more was lovingly stitched on table linen and bed linen. King David Street is the best place to look for antiques.

Handicrafts

Tooled camel-hide bags and cushions, olive wood carvings and boxes inlaid with mother of pearl abound in the Old City, where there are also excellent examples of basketware, much of it produced by the blind. The best camel-hide products are sold by the shops in the Christian

Quarter. At the **House of Quality** at 12 Hebron Road, a complex of studios and showrooms outside the Old City walls, there is a fascinating choice of pottery and metal items.

Ritual Objects

Because Jerusalem is a pilgrim city, her artists and artisans must constantly tax their imagination to produce something new and different for ritual purposes. Nowhere in the world, not even in Rome, will you see so many varieties of Madonna and Child or so many different kinds of crucifix or Nativity crib sets carved from olive wood. The broad spectrum of articles on display for the Jewish market is quite mind-boggling. The greatest effort goes into the designing of *mezuza* cases and the eight-branched candelabra used for the festival of Hanukka. A *mezuza* is a small case containing a scroll with verses from the *Book of Deuteronomy*. It is affixed by Jews to their doorposts. There isn't a commercial centre anywhere in Israel, including the Arab sector of East Jerusalem, where there isn't some type of Jewish ritual object for sale. The best choice of likely items is to be found in Me'a She'arim.

ACCOMMODATION

Jerusalem offers accommodation to suit every budget. As in nearly every other city around the globe, prices vary between high and low seasons. Prices for groups, whether in 5-star *de-luxe* hotels, youth hostels or religious hospices are always cheaper than for the individual traveller. The difference can be as much as 20 or 30 per cent. Prices in the Old City and the other parts of East Jerusalem tend to be lower than those of West Jerusalem, though many tourists, wary of being caught in the occasional political unrest of East Jerusalem, prefer to stay in the western part of the city. Possible exceptions are the Seven Arches and the Hyatt hotels. Visitors who come on package deal group tours will find that both these high quality hotels are reasonably priced, but those who come as foreign individual tourists, without having made their reservations through an overseas travel agency or reservations service, will have to pay a significantly higher rate. Many bargain rate deals offered by 4- and 5-star hotels are valid only when the reservation has been made from abroad.

Peak periods in both East and West Jerusalem are generally from March to May and late September to the end of October; also around Christmas. For the most part only hotels in the Western sector have higher rates during peak periods. Visitors who prefer the more rustic environment of the *kibbutz* (communal settlement) or *moshav* (cooperative settlement) can take advantage of attractive hotel-style accommodation at several such settlements which are between 15 and 25 minutes' drive from the central hub of the city.

Another option is camping. There is a handful of well-equipped sites on the outskirts of the city.

Although it is fairly easy to get accommodation in Jerusalem by just walking in off the street, it is advisable to make a reservation through your travel agent, who may be able to wangle a better financial deal for you from your home country. Remember when paying the bill that payments in internationally accepted foreign currencies are free of Value Added Tax (VAT).

Some of the Old City's small hotels and hostels are located inside the labyrinth of winding alleyways which are too narrow to permit the passage of cars or buses. Pilgrim groups utilising such facilities are usually brought by bus to the Jaffa Gate, where they wait with their luggage for a spare donkey to take the suitcases. Sometimes the cases are loaded onto a trolley which is either pulled by a donkey or pushed by two or three young boys. There are stone benches near the Jaffa Gate, which makes the wait less tiring. Although this may not be the best means of introduction to the city, it does help to give pilgrims a sense of familiarity with their surroundings in comparison to those tourists who are whisked straight from the airport to their hotels.

A swimming pool and health spa are among the many facilities at the 5-star Hyatt Regency Hotel

Expensive

Hyatt Regency, 32 Lehi Street (tel: 821 333). One of the most beautifully designed hotels in Jerusalem, the Hyatt is located outside the city centre on the slopes of Mount Scopus. It is within easy walking distance of the Hebrew University campus, the Mount Scopus division of the Hadassah Hospital and the Commonwealth War Graves Cemetery. Vegetarians will enjoy dining at Valentino's, the Hyatt's Italian-style dairy restaurant. The hotel runs an hourly shuttle service to and from the down-town area. There are also regular bus routes close to the hotel and a taxi service which operates from the hotel grounds. The well-equipped Hyatt Health Spa is an added attraction.

King David, 32 David haMelekh (King David) Street (tel: 251 111). A status symbol in Jerusalem since the period of the British Mandate, the King David exudes an old world elegance. Royalty and world leaders who stay in Jerusalem overnight are almost invariably guests here. The back of the hotel, with its spacious gardens, overlooks the glorious panorama of the Old City, which is within easy walking distance. In summertime, guests like to sit on the hotel's patio where they can appreciate both the garden and the view. The hotel, because of its place in the development of the history of modern Israel, is a tourist attraction in its own right.

Moderately Expensive

American Colony, Nablus Road (tel: 282 421/2/3). On any day of the year, the American Colony Hotel will have at least two or three journalists among its guests. When events of world-shattering importance are taking place in Jerusalem, the hotel takes on the appearance of a residential Foreign Press Club. It has also become a semi-official meeting place between visiting statesmen and politicians and leaders of the Palestinian community. But aside from all this, its charm lies in its authentic Middle Eastern ambience. In addition, tourists who prefer a sense of luxury but don't want to be restricted by Jewish dietary laws, choose the American Colony.

Jerusalem Hilton, Giv'at Ram (tel: 536 151). To the traveller coming up the main highway to Jerusalem, the first real sign that the destination is within sight is the multi-storey Jerusalem Hilton. It is especially popular among convention groups due to its proximity to the Jerusalem Convention Centre, and is also conveniently close to the Central Bus Station and the El Al terminal.

Laromme, 3 Jabotinsky Street (tel: 697 777). An extremely attractive building, constructed around an open courtyard, the Laromme benefits from a great deal of natural light. In the summer months the courtyard is used for weddings and other social events. The hotel borders the sprawling Liberty Bell Garden with its playgrounds and Train Theatre for children and small amphitheatre for adults. The hotel is close to several bus routes and within easy walking distance of the Old City.

Moriah, 39 Keren haYessod Street (tel: 232 232). Located just around the corner from the King David. One of the reasons for the Moriah's popularity is the volume and variety of guest activities. The hotel has built a reputation on returning guests, and has done this by creating a family atmosphere in which guests do not feel like strangers.

Ramada Renaissance, 6 Wolfson Street (tel: 528 111). The largest hotel in Israel, the twin-tower Ramada Renaissance has its own comprehensive convention facilities. Despite its size, it does have a degree of intimacy. It is close to the National Library, the Israel Museum and the Knesset on one side and the entrance to the city and the Central Bus station on the other.

Seven Arches, Mount of Olives (tel: 894 455). To the pilgrim, this hotel with its widely praised (non-kosher) cuisine, is a springboard to both Old Testament and New Testament history, standing as it does at the top of the Mount of Olives and overlooking the vista of the Old City. Souvenir hawkers line the roadway outside the hotel and a camel patiently hoists tourists on its back so that they can pose for photos. Public transport facilities to the top of the Mount of Olives are unfortunately scarce and infrequent.

Sheraton Jerusalem Plaza, 47 HaMelekh George (King George) Street (tel: 228 133). The Sheraton Plaza is favoured by Jewish visitors to Jerusalem because it is located across the road from the Jewish Agency, the Great Synagogue and Keren haKayemet Street. The hotel,

which is one bus stop away from down-town, sits on the edge of Independence Park.

Reasonably Priced

Mount Zion, 17 Hebron Road (tel: 724 222). With spectacular views, this is very close to the House of Quality, in which some of the best artists and artisans have their studios, and within easy walking distance of the Jerusalem Cinematheque, Yemin Moshe and the Liberty Bell Garden.

National Palace, 4 Az Zahara Street (tel: 273 273). Here the visitor is assailed by the pungent aromas which lend an exotic air to East Jerusalem. Some of these aromas emanate from the hotel's own kitchen: the cuisine has a good reputation. The hotel is conveniently close to a variety of shops.

Tirat Batsheva, 42 HaMelekh George (King George) Street (tel: 232 121). This relatively small, attractive hotel on the very edge of down-town Jerusalem was recently refurbished. Nearly all the rooms have private balconies. The hotel also has an excellent restaurant whose menu is ideal for the calorie-conscious.

Windmill, 3 Mendele Street (tel: 663 111). An extremely popular hotel, conveniently tucked away in a side street within easy walking distance of a main highway, but removed from the bustle and noise. Because its public areas are relatively small and intimate, the establishment has a family atmosphere. Unlike the nearby Moriah and Laromme hotels, it does not have a swimming pool.

YMCA, 26 David haMelekh (King David) Street (tel: 227 111). To stay at the 'Y' is to live in majestic surroundings. The building itself has a definite 19th-century grandeur, with an elegant, large dining terrace. The 'Y', which does not observe the Jewish dietary laws, is a hub of sporting, cultural, social and spiritual activity in which Jews, Christians and Muslims come together on a regular basis. If any place in Israel can demonstrate the feasibility of coexistence at all levels, it is the 'Y'. It is one of the very few hotels in which visitors can come into contact with the local population on a regular basis. The 'Y' is not just for tourists—it is integral to the community.

Budget
Holyland East, 6 Reshid Street (tel: 284 841). Located in the centre of East Jerusalem, this pleasant hotel and its neighbours have suffered low occupancies ever since the start of the *intifada* towards the end of 1987. The truth is that there is very little justification for bypassing hotels in East Jerusalem. Their bed-and-breakfast rates are all lower than those of hotels in West Jerusalem, their service is courteous, and for the most part, the food is good. Certainly for anyone who wants to get the Arab flavour of the city and who wants to be a few minutes' walk away from the Damascus Gate, East Jerusalem hotels are recommended.
Palatin, 4 Agrippas Street (tel: 231 141). Recently renovated and located in the very heart of down-town Jerusalem, this small,

The YMCA – its grand buildings are a centre of activity for tourists and the local community alike

intimate 2-star hotel offers a family plan for visitors on a tight budget. There are telephones in all the rooms, but no radio or TV.
Pilgrims Palace, Sultan Suleiman Street (tel: 284 831). Almost facing the Damascus Gate, the hotel's comfortable lobby-lounge offers an excellent vantage point for those wishing to observe the hustle and bustle of life in East Jerusalem. The hotel will provide television in rooms on request. It has a good dining room, banquet facilities and meeting rooms.

ACCOMMODATION

Recreation Centre, Jerusalem Forest (tel: 416 060). This is an ideal place for someone who wants to get away from it all and be close to nature, with all the comforts of home, plus swimming pool, tennis court and television.

Youth Hostels

The title is somewhat misleading since so many hostels also have an adult clientele. Most hostels offer bed and breakfast in dormitory-style facilities in which there are four to six beds. Newer facilities, such as **Bet Shemu'el**, which is part of the Hebrew Union College complex, also have *en suite* toilets and showers and charge slightly more for lodgings. The youth hostels are affiliated to the Israel Youth Hostel Association at 3 Dorot Harishonim Street (off the Ben Yehuda Mall) (tel: 222 073), which in turn is affiliated to the International Youth Hostel Association (IYHA).

Christian Hospices

With one or two exceptions,

Christian hospices and youth hostels offer cheap accommodation. Above, an Old City youth hostel

these offer the least expensive accommodation. Most of the hospices also provide meals at an extra charge. Lodgings, though somewhat stark in some places, are clean and comfortable. Understandably, those hospices which have shower and toilet facilities attached to the rooms charge more. Dormitory facilities are considerably cheaper than single or double rooms, but some dormitories afford little or no privacy and have as many as 40 beds in them. One need not be a pilgrim or a Christian to stay in any of these hospices. A selection of hospices follows. A fuller list may be obtained through the Ministry of Tourism or from the Christian Information Service inside the Jaffa Gate. **Christ Church Hospice**, Jaffa Gate (tel: 282 082); Anglican. Four single rooms, 16 2-beds, two 3-beds, three 4-beds, and dormitories. All rooms with shower and toilet facilities. Reduced rates for children and for groups of 20 or more.

Ecce Homo Convent, Via Dolorosa (tel: 282 445); Roman Catholic. 12 single rooms (two with bath), 21 double rooms (15 with bath), five triple rooms (four with bath), 23 single cubicles in dormitory plus 35-bed dormitory. Bed and breakfast; full board and half board arrangements are also available. This hospice has an excellent reputation both for its hospitality and its work in fostering peaceful relations among people of different faiths and nationalities.

Franciscaines de Marie ('White Sisters'), 9 Nablus Road (tel: 282 633). The Roman Catholic nuns have a 40-bed dormitory for women only plus one 3-bed room, 23 double rooms and three single rooms with shower and toilet; bed and breakfast. Other meals are optional.

Notre Dame de France, Opposite New Gate (tel: 289 723); Roman Catholic. A place of history and grandeur, the hospice is actually a 140-room hotel. Most of the rooms are doubles, but there are a few singles available. All have *en suite* bathrooms and new, modern furniture. The hotel is located in the grounds of the magnificent Notre Dame Cathedral, and boasts one of the finest dining rooms in Israel. Bed and breakfast, half board and full board options are available. Hotel prices are seasonally adjusted.

Rosary Convent Hostel, 14 Agron Street (tel: 228 529); Roman

Catholic. Bed only; bed and breakfast, half board and full board by arrangement. The convent can accommodate 49 guests in one single room, eight 2-bed rooms, eight 3-bed rooms and two 4-bed rooms.

St Andrews Scots Memorial Hospice, Rakevet Street (near Cinematheque) (tel: 717 701); Church of Scotland. Seven single rooms, eight double rooms, two family rooms. Bed and breakfast; dinner is optional.

St George's Hostel, 20 Nablus Road (tel: 283 302); Anglican. This is a small hospice with two single rooms, nine double rooms and two 3-bed rooms offering bed and breakfast, half board or full board.

Kibbutz Hotels

In the early years of the State of Israel, it was virtually taboo for most *kibbutzim* to operate a guesthouse, let alone a hotel. But over the years, *kibbutz* philosophy, tempered by economic hardship, has changed. Many *kibbutzim* established industries such as the production of irrigation equipment, furniture, plastics, clothing, etc. In addition, they also began to charge for hospitality. Initially they rented out a few rooms or apartments not yet occupied by *kibbutz* members. Then they built guesthouses and more recently have constructed proper hotels. The *moshavim* (cooperative settlements) were quick to jump on the bandwagon, and they too reap a respectable income from hosting domestic and foreign tourists. *Kibbutzim* and *moshavim* with hotel facilities are located within 15–20 minutes' drive from Jerusalem. All are air-conditioned and have swimming pools and tennis courts. All operate in a rural environment. They include **Kiryat Anavim** (tel: 348 999) 93 rooms, **Maaleh Hahamisha** (tel: 342 591) 121 rooms, **Neve Ilan** (tel: 341 241) 80 rooms, **Mitzpeh Rachel** (tel: 702 555) 79 rooms, **Shoresh** (tel: 341 171) 114 rooms.

Camping (see also **Directory)**

Israel is an excellent country for camping. Most sites offer full sanitary facilities, electricity, restaurant, shop, shaded picnic and camp-fire areas and 24-hour security. Sites in the vicinity of Jerusalem include:
Bet Zayit (tel: 346 217). In wooded hills about 3 miles (5km) west of the city.
Ein Hemed (Aqua Bella) (tel: 342 741). In national park, about 6 miles (10km) west of Jerusalem, off the Tel Aviv highway.
Ramat Rahel (tel: 702 555). Situated on the edge of Jerusalem. Good bus service to the city.

CULTURE, ENTERTAINMENT, NIGHTLIFE

Considering the size of its population, Jerusalem has an extraordinarily rich cultural and social life running the whole gamut from low-brow to high-brow. See **Entertainment Information** in **Directory** for where to find details of the entertainments listed.
Many plays, lectures etc are held in the English language. The overwhelming majority of the city's entertainment outlets are set in clusters, so if one place doesn't look as good as it seemed in an advertisement, there are at least three or four alternatives within a few minutes' walk. Visitors to the Khan, for instance, are very close to The Sixth Place, the Cinematheque, Cannibal, the YMCA and the King David Hotel as well as a string of restaurants in Keren Hayesod and King David Streets. Then again, it is less than 10 minutes' walk from the King David Hotel to that section of Jaffa Road with the highest proliferation of restaurants and bars. The Talpiot Industrial Zone (bus 14) and 'Emeq Refa'im (buses 4, 14) are both popular restaurant and entertainment areas.

Art Exhibitions

There is certainly no dearth of galleries in Jerusalem, especially in and around King David Street. A comprehensive list of galleries appears in *This Week in Jerusalem*, available free of charge at hotel reception desks and at Ministry of Tourism Information offices.

Cinema/Video

With the exception of school holiday periods, cinemas operate only in the late afternoons and evenings. During school holidays they also have morning screenings. The **Cinematheque** also has midnight screenings on Thursdays. The Cinematheque screens films from all over the world; holds an annual film festival in June or July; operates a film library; and has an excellent restaurant serving light meals. There is an exceptional view from the

terrace of the restaurant.
Legend, 4 Shamai Street (tel: 233 253), Restaurant Bar and Grill has six video screens dedicated to American sports, news and entertainment. Programmes are 24 hours behind those shown in the USA.
Lynch Pub, 17 Jaffa Road, features experimental films.

Dancing
Ballroom Dancing
Knesset Tower Hotel
Switch Club, Lev Yerushalayim, 31 Hillel Street
Folk dancing is extremely popular in Israel and is taught on a regular basis in nearly all community centres. Visitors to Jerusalem who would rather watch than participate should scan the posters in their hotel lobbies where the **International Cultural Centre for Youth**, 12a 'Emeq Refa'im (tel: 664 144) announces dates and times of performances. The ICCY also conducts classes in folk dancing. Another folklore outlet is the **Khan** at 2 David Remez Square. The Khan complex includes a theatre, restaurant, folklore entertainment for tourists and an intimate disco and piano bar. Jewish and Arab folklore recitals can be seen on Monday, Thursday and Saturday nights at the **YMCA**, 26 King David Street, (tel: 227 111)

Nightclubs, Bars and Pubs
Yad Harutzim Street in the Talpiot Industrial Zone, 15 minutes from downtown Jerusalem, has become a popular area for late-night entertainment. Clubs open and close in rapid succession, but do not disappear from the scene.

Just take note of the flashing neon and the sound of music. Pubs and bars with recorded or live entertainment also abound, particularly in down-town Rivlin and Yoel Salomon Streets and the web of side streets running off both.
Other than 5-star hotel bars, there are no really up-market bars, pubs or nightclubs in Jerusalem. Most clubs, as previously mentioned, are in the Talpiot Industrial Zone, although there are others in some hotels and down-town in and around that part of Jaffa Road which is situated between Zion Square and the Jaffa Gate.
While there are many restaurants in East Jerusalem, there are very few bars or pubs owing to the Islamic prohibition against the consumption of alcohol. Most of the nightlife and entertainment outlets are in West Jerusalem.

The Performing Arts
Classical music: The Jerusalem Symphony Orchestra has its home platform in the acoustically perfect Henry Crown Auditorium at the **Jerusalem Centre for the Performing Arts**. As yet, Jerusalem does not have an opera house, but this will be remedied in the course of time.
The Jerusalem Music Centre at Mishkenot Sha'ananim is certainly worth a visit. The Music Centre, which encourages musical talent, has, in addition to its regular concerts, a Master Class programme pioneered by the violin virtuoso Isaac Stern. Poetry readings, art exhibitions and concerts are held quite frequently in the public areas of

Live entertainment under the stars, at The Sultan's Pool

Mishkenot Sha'ananim. **Tzavta** at 38 King George Street (tel: 227 621), aware of how little there is to do in Jerusalem on a Saturday morning, holds classical music recitals at 11:00 A.M. on Saturdays in its tiny theatre. Further out of town, at the same time on Saturdays, the **Targ Music Centre** in 'En Karem (tel: 414 250) has chamber music recitals. Classical afternoon concerts are held at 4:00 P.M. on Thursdays at the **YMCA** in King David Street (tel: 227 111). The **Redeemer Church** in the Old City (tel: 282 543) holds Saturday night organ recitals. **Folk music** from different countries is played on Friday nights at **Bet Shemu'el** 6 Shamai Street (tel: 203 456), with other cultural events—some of them in English—on other nights. **Jazz** lovers congregate at lunch time each Friday at the intimate Pargod Theatre at 94 Bezalel Street (tel: 231 765) for a three to four hour jam session. There are also jazz concerts at night on other days of the week, as well as cabaret, rock and experimental theatre. The **Sultan's Pool** is an outdoor venue attracting thousands. **Advance tickets for concerts and theatrical productions** can be purchased at **Ben Naim**, 38 Jaffa Road (tel: 224 008); **Bimot**, 8 Shamai Street (tel: 240 896); **Kahana**, 1 Dorot Rishonim Street (tel: 222 831) and **Klaim**, 16 Shamai Street (tel: 221 624).

Poetry Evenings and Lectures
The Zionist Confederation House in Emile Botta Street which runs along the side of the King David Hotel, holds lectures and poetry evenings every week. There is a restaurant on the premises, so there is no need to rush to grab a meal in town or at your hotel. These and other English-language activities are advertised in tourist publications on display at hotel reception desks and in *In Jerusalem*, the Friday supplement of *The Jerusalem Post*.

Sound and Light Show
Nightly except Friday, Tower of David.

WEATHER AND WHEN TO GO

Religion plays an important part in determining when to visit Jerusalem. For Christians the most important times are Easter and Christmas. The Easter procession with its colourful and spiritually moving services, and the Christmas procession from Jerusalem to Bethlehem are both emotionally indelible experiences for Christians.
For Muslims, Mohammed's birthday, Id El-Fidr and Id El-Adha are the most important times. Their exact dates cannot be pinpointed on the Gregorian calendar, as Muslims observe a lunar calendar.
Jews too observe a lunar calendar which, in a leap year, includes not just an extra day, as in the Gregorian calendar, but a whole month. For Jews there are both religious and national holidays to celebrate. The most

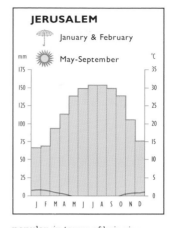

JERUSALEM

January & February

May-September

popular, in terms of bringing visitors to Israel, are Pessach (Passover) and Rosh Hashana (Jewish New Year). Pessach usually falls some time in April, which is the beginning of spring. The weather is a little windy, but the days are pleasantly warm. The evenings are cold. The visitor who spends six weeks in Jerusalem beginning in mid-March, will in all probability celebrate Easter, Pessach and Mohammed's birthday.
Rosh Hashana, which falls in September/October, ushers in over three weeks of festivals. Rosh Hashana itself is a two-day festival, followed ten days later by Yom Kippur (the Day of Atonement), Succot (Tabernacles) and Simchat Torah.
Technically speaking, Rosh Hashana marks the beginning of autumn, but the weather is not the least bit autumnal. Day-time temperatures are 68°F (20°C) and higher and the evenings are pleasantly mild, though

occasionally cool.

Most buildings are well heated in winter and air-conditioned in summer. Jerusalem has more hot days than cold days throughout the year. The cold period, with occasional days of rain and hail, begins around mid-November and continues through till March. Weather conditions are neither constant nor consistent. A cold, blustering, rainy day can be followed or preceded by brilliant sunshine. Very often the day may start out wintry and end up summery, or vice versa. Snow is a rare experience in Jerusalem, and when it does fall at any time between the end of December and mid March it quickly turns to slush.

Anyone coming to Jerusalem at this time has real problems in deciding what to pack. The best idea is to concentrate on a mainly lightweight wardrobe, plus a very warm jacket, a cardigan and/or a sweater. Thermal underwear would also help on the colder days, but when the weather is playing havoc it is much easier to remove an outer garment when the sun comes out.

April and May are warm but windy. June, July, August and September are very hot months in which temperatures may average around 75–80°F (24–26°C). Jerusalem used to have a dry heat, but with the passing of the years, the weather has become somewhat erratic, and there are days when the climate is more humid than that of Tel Aviv, which has a reputation for humidity.

Weather reports are given on the radio and television each day, as well as in *The Jerusalem Post*, the English language daily. Fog occasionally descends on the city in the winter months; and in summer, the brightness of the sun is often a hazard to motorists. The city is plagued by dust all year round.

Clothing

Bearing in mind that most buildings are well-heated in winter, lightweight clothes are essential at all times of the year. Jerusalemites are very casual, and even elegant, 5-star hotels seldom demand that a guest wears a jacket and tie in the dining area. However, they will not permit people to walk through the lobbies in a state of undress. That means anyone coming through from the swimming pool must cover their upper torso.

It is important to include some form of headgear in one's luggage, especially in summer, but also in order not to offend. Visitors to the Western Wall and other Jewish religious sites are asked, as a sign of respect, to cover their heads. This does not apply to unmarried women.

HOW TO BE A LOCAL

Other than in the strictly orthodox Jewish and Arab sectors of Jerusalem, there are no traditional ways of behaviour. Because the Arabs set great store by hospitality, it is impolite to refuse to take any food or drink.

In the ultra-orthodox Jewish neighbourhoods of Me'a She'arim and Geula, it is unwise for women to wear skimpy clothes. The residents of these two adjoining neighbourhoods have put large signs on the walls asking women not to enter if they are immodestly dressed. Immodesty in their definition includes all unseemly exposure of the human body. This means that their own women wear sleeves which are at least elbow length; skirts which come well below the knee; and necklines which are no lower than the collar bone. Married women keep their heads covered with kerchiefs, snoods, turbans or wigs. Very few women in these neighbourhoods go bare-legged. Most wear thick stockings. Jeans and similar garb are frowned on because they are too form-fitting. Immodestly clad women who venture into Me'a She'arim run the risk of being physically attacked.

All men in these neighbourhoods keep their heads covered, either with a hat or skull-cap known as a *kippa* in Hebrew or *yarmulke* in Yiddish. Any male wandering bare-headed through these areas is automatically recognised as a stranger. The overwhelming majority of males wear dark suits with white shirts, and some, instead of a suit jacket, wear a fitted coat known as a *kapote*. On the Sabbath and other Jewish holy days, male headgear among married men becomes far more luxurious. Some wear a *shtreimel* which is a flattish velvet hat lavishly trimmed with fur; and others wear a *spodek*, which is a high-standing cap fashioned from short-haired fur. Ultra-orthodox men do not as a rule shake hands with women. When being introduced, it is

Time for a chat ...

wiser for women not to proffer their hands, because more often than not the gesture will be ignored.

When dining in any observant Jewish home, don't ask for milk in your tea or coffee if you've had a meat meal. It goes against Jewish dietary laws.

Neither very orthodox Jews nor Muslims are happy about mixing socially with people of other religions. They will entertain people of other faiths in their homes, but will seldom allow their children to socialise with their peers of another faith for fear of undue influence, and worse still, the development of a romance which could lead to intermarriage.

Israelis are generally very brash and don't hesitate to ask your age, your income, how much you paid for your house and whether you're having an extra-marital relationship—so don't be shocked if these subjects crop up at the dinner table.

When eating in a Jewish religious household, grace is recited before and after meals. If there is no bread on the table, individual grace is recited over each course. If bread is broken, there is no need for further blessings till the end of the meal. Prior to the eating of the bread, there is a ritual hand-washing ceremony, in which water is poured from a ewer three times on each hand. It is customary to remove rings prior to the hand-washing ceremony. There is no conversation between the ceremony and the prayer recited over the bread. In some households, the host will slice the bread, dip it in salt and pass it around the table.

If you are a Sabbath guest in a religious Jewish home, refrain from smoking and keep your hands away from the light switches. Orthodox Jews are not permitted to create or extinguish fire or electricity on the Sabbath, nor are they allowed to directly ask a non-Jew to do it for them. They may, however, hint at it if the need arises, and the non-Jewish guest can respond favourably to the hint, without offending.

PERSONAL PRIORITIES

Generally, visitors will have few difficulties in obtaining toiletries, but non-Israeli brands manufactured outside the country—such as Tampax or Colgate, for example—can be considerably more expensive than Israeli brands; you may want to take supplies of your own to be on the safe side. Items such as contraceptives and diapers are easily available—see **Directory**, under **Pharmacist**, for the addresses of outlets.

Women rarely travel alone in Israel, but there is seldom a threatening atmosphere, either in Jewish or Arab sectors of the city. Mugging and violence are relatively rare, but theft is common (see **Directory**, under **Personal Safety**). Families usually have no qualms about letting their children and teenagers go out alone in Jerusalem; they are considered safer here than in many other busy cities.

Visitors will find that a good deal of drinking and socialising is done in the hotel bars, and those who do go out will find that most of Jerusalem is pretty liberal: except among the more orthodox communities, there is an air of toleration and acceptance of the unconventional.

CHILDREN

There is no dearth of activities for children in Jerusalem. A special Youth Wing at the **Israel Museum** organises a broad range of activities for children of all ages (tel: 698 211 for details). **Ann's House** at 14 Shoshana

Street, Kiryat Moshe, has regular singing, dancing and storytime programmes in English (tel: 525 604). The **Train Theatre**, situated in the Liberty Bell Garden, has daily productions for children.

The **Jerusalem Biblical Zoo** at Yermiyahu Street in the Romema neighbourhood contains most of the animals mentioned in the Bible. The zoo is open from 9:00 A.M. to sunset. It is also open on Saturdays, but tickets for entry on Saturdays must be purchased in advance. For further information telephone 814 822 or 811 334. During the summer months, most 4- and 5-star hotels conduct summer camps for children to enable adult guests to go off by themselves.

Liberty Bell Park – fun for children in one of Israel's most attractive public gardens

TIGHT BUDGET

At first glance, Jerusalem may not seem the easiest place in the world to stay on a tight budget but there are many opportunities for savings to be made.

Some travellers find it cheaper to take a round trip flight from their countries of origin to Cairo in Egypt, and then to continue overland by bus to Jerusalem, which takes between 12 and 14 hours. Bus fares inside Jerusalem are very reasonably priced, considerably lower than those in most countries in the Western world. The Jerusalem bus service is excellent. But there are so many interesting things to see in Jerusalem that most visitors spurn the bus unless they are tired, in a hurry, or their destination is in an outlying suburb.

For inexpensive accommodation, it is advisable to

contact the Israel Youth Hostel Association or one of the Christian Hospices (listed under **Accommodation**). Visitors planning to spend a month or more in Israel will find it cheaper to rent an apartment and to commute from Jerusalem to other parts of the country, than to take pot luck when travelling from place to place. It is also much more comfortable and convenient for backpackers travelling in groups of two to six to rent an apartment jointly and to have somewhere to deposit their belongings while they explore the country.

Jerusalem is a tourist city. There are free guided tours advertised in English on city billboards and in tourist publications available gratis at hotel reception desks and from Ministry of Tourism and Municipal Information Offices. Enquiries can also be made at the Christian Information Office. See under **Tourist Offices** in the **Directory** section for details of the opening times, addresses and telephone numbers of these offices.

There are numerous exhibitions and museums where entry is either free of charge, nominal or by donation. These include: Arts and Crafts Lane, Franciscan Biblical Museum, Herzl Museum, Jerusalem Artists' House, Museum of Jewish Art, Natural History Museum, Palestinian Arab Folklore Centre, Palombo Museum, Skirball Museum, Taxation Museum, The American Colony Hotel, Ticho House and Yad Vashem. See **Museums** section of **What To See** for details.

SPECIAL EVENTS AND FESTIVALS

Jewish Religion and Festivals

Since close to 80 per cent of the population of Israel is Jewish, the general emphasis on the way of life and on national holidays and days of mourning is dictated by Jewish tradition.

Due to time differences between Israel and the rest of the world, some holy days which are celebrated for only one day in Israel are celebrated for two days abroad. This enables the time of celebration to coincide with Israeli real time in addition to taking in the considerations of local time. Religiously observant Jews who visit Israel during these holy days continue to observe two days as a sign that they are not residents of Israel. Jewish festivals and holy days are linked to feasting or fasting. The major festivals and days of mourning are mentioned below. It is impossible to list exact Gregorian calendar dates; the Jewish calendar is lunar and there is an extra month in a leap year.

For Muslim and Christian festivals, see **Holidays** in **Directory**.

The origins of most Jewish festivals are to be found in the first five books of the Bible.

January/February

Tu B'Shvat New Year for Trees: This is the 15th day in the Hebrew calendar month of Shvat. On this particular day schoolchildren all over Israel visit forests to plant new saplings. The main tree planting

Children in fancy dress celebrate the Jewish festival of Purim

ceremony in Jerusalem takes place in the Jerusalem Peace Forest. On Tu B'Shvat fruit dominates the menu, and in some households the meal must consist of at least 15 different kinds of fruits.

March/April

Purim: The background to this festival can be gleaned from reading the biblical *Book of Esther*. The festival itself commemorates the deliverance of the Jews of Shushan from annihilation. Haman, the king's chief adviser, plotted to get rid of them, but his plan was foiled by Esther, the king's consort, and Mordechai, her uncle. The festival is celebrated on the 15th day of the Hebrew calendar month of Adar. There is a carnival atmosphere in which children dress up in fancy costumes. It is customary to eat triangular shaped pastries called *oznei Haman*, which translates literally as Haman's ears.

Pessach: Often coinciding with Easter, this commemorates the Exodus of the ancient Children of Israel from Egypt and is known as Passover in English. In their haste to escape the Egyptians, the ancient Israelites had no time to wait for their bread to rise, and in remembrance of this period of unleavened bread, Jews remove all signs of leaven from their homes.

Mimouna: Originating in North Africa, this celebration is held on the day after Pessach. People from all over the country converge on Jerusalem's Sacher Park where the pungent aroma of barbecued meats fills the air.

Martyrs' Remembrance Day: The date chosen by Israel to remember the six million Jewish martyrs who lost their lives in the Holocaust is that of the Warsaw Ghetto Uprising of 1943. The key ceremony is held at Yad Vashem.

Remembrance Day for the Fallen Soldiers in Israel's Wars: The solemn ceremony is held at the plaza adjacent to the Western

Wall of the Old City. Services are held at military cemeteries throughout the country during the day.

Independence Day: Celebrates the anniversary of the declaration of the establishment of the sovereign state of Israel. The streets are absolutely packed with people. Some 20 years ago, some unknown person decided that Independence Day celebrations would be incomplete without plastic hammers. Vendors start selling these noisy but painless implements halfway through Remembrance Day, and people bop each other on the head.

May/June

Lag B'Omer: The 33rd day after Passover. The Omer is a measure of grain, symbolically counted for 49 days from the second night of Passover and culminating in the festival of Shavuot (Pentecost). These seven weeks evolved into a period of semi-mourning in which weddings, the playing of musical instruments and the cutting of hair were forbidden. According to Jewish tradition, a terrible plague which swept through the land is believed to have stopped on the 33rd day of the counting of the Omer. In religious circles it is customary to give a male child his first haircut on Lag B'Omer. The event is accompanied by great feasting and merry-making. This is also the most popular day of the year for weddings.

Jerusalem Day, which is also celebrated according to its Hebrew calendar date, is a modern holiday dating back to June 1967, when the divided city of Jerusalem was reunified. Jerusalem Day draws people from all over the country to the capital. Many come to join the parade through the main streets.

Shavuot (Pentecost): The festival of weeks, marking the end of the 49 days of the counting of the Omer (see above). A harvest festival, Shavuot is one of the three pilgrim festivals mentioned in the Bible. Aside from the harvest, this festival also marks the descent of Moses from Mount Sinai. In modern Israel, the synagogues are decorated with plants and flowers. On the day preceding the festival children come to school with garlands on their heads and around their necks.

July/August

Jerusalem Film Festival: This week-long festival is held annually in June or July.

Tisha B'Av: The ninth day of the month of Av is the date, over a period of many centuries, that several terrible calamities befell the Jewish people. The worst of these was the destruction by the Babylonians in 586BC of the First Temple in Jerusalem. On the same date in AD70, Titus burned down the Second Temple. In AD135, the revolt against the Romans ended on Tisha B'Av with the fall of the fortress of Bethar. The date is marked by a 25-hour period of fasting and prayer. Thousands of people gather at Jerusalem's Wailing Wall to read from the *Book of Lamentations*.

The Israel Festival: This has absolute nothing to do with religion. The month-long festival incorporates all the performing arts, and provides a stage for individual and group performers from Israel and abroad. The festival includes street theatre.

September/October
Rosh Hashana: The Jewish New Year, this actually falls in the seventh month of the Jewish year. Just as the seventh day is regarded as the holiest day of the week, so the seventh month, the month of Tishrei, is regarded as the holiest month of the year; indeed, there are more holy days in this month than in any other. Rosh Hashana is a time in which each Jew takes stock of himself: it is a day of judgement. In the afternoon of the first day of the New Year (or the second day if the first day falls on a Sabbath), religious families go to the seashore to pray and symbolically cast away their sins. Because Jerusalem does not have a seashore, those people who observe the tradition of casting out their sins go either to the spring of Shiloah in the City of David or to the wells in Me'a She'arim.

Yom Kippur: This comes ten days after Rosh Hashana and is the Day of Atonement, the most solemn day in the year. Yom Kippur is marked primarily by fasting and prayer. The streets of West Jerusalem are almost devoid of motorised traffic and the synagogues are full. Shops and restaurants are closed.

Succot (Tabernacles): This is celebrated four days after Yom Kippur. It is a thanksgiving festival for the harvest and for the mercies rendered to the Children of Israel during their 40

A menorah for Hanukka, *the Jewish Festival of Lights*

years of wandering in the wilderness. The building of the *succa*, the booth or tabernacle, begins immediately after the end of Yom Kippur.

Simchat Torah: This is the rejoicing of the Law, at the end of Succot, and crowns this holiday period. The final reading is concluded of the Torah scroll, on which is transcribed the first five books of the bible, containing the body of Jewish law, and the scroll is wound back to start again with the first chapter of the *Book of Genesis*.

On the night after Simchat Torah, a semi-religious celebration is held at the Liberty Bell Garden.

November/December
Hanukka: The Festival of Lights, a minor festival, though it commemorates a major miracle. After the desecration of the Temple only one small vessel of

ritual oil remained sufficient to give light for one day. However, when Mattathias and his sons had purified the Temple, this oil burned for eight days. Eight-branched candelabra are lit to bear witness to the miracle.

Christmas: In Jerusalem this is somewhat of a disappointment to the Christian visitor. The principal Christmas celebration is in Beth-lehem's Church of the Nativity and Manger Square, some 10–15 minutes' drive from Jerusalem.

SPORTS

Jerusalem's sporting activities are somewhat hampered by the religious Jewish factions who for several years now have stood in the way of the construction of a world-class soccer stadium. None the less, soccer has developed, along with many other sports brought to Jerusalem from other parts of the globe: British, South African, Australian, American and Indian immigrants have introduced such games as cricket, hockey, rugby, baseball, softball and, most recently, American touch football. Tennis acquired great popularity in the 1970s, and has become increasingly popular as more and more schoolchildren take up the game. There are swimming pools in all 5-star and most 4-star hotels, as well as in Ramat Rachel, the YMCA in West Jerusalem, the YMHA at 105 Herzog Street, the Jerusalem Spa at the Hyatt Hotel, with its own separate facility, Kiryat Hayovel and 'Emeq Refa'im. Pools are also to be found at several *kibbutzim* and *moshavim* within 15–20 minutes' drives of

the centre of Jerusalem. Most of these settlements also have tennis and basketball courts. Neve Ilan also caters to equestrians. Squash enthusiasts can catch up on their game at the Acadomon Sports Building at the Giv'at Ram Campus of the Hebrew University, where they can also watch American sports on video. Video-taped American sports can also be seen at the American Cultural Centre at 19 Keren haYessod Street.

Quite a number of sporting activities in Jerusalem are run without benefit of a regular meeting place. They are conducted at the initiative of various enthusiasts.

The sports which follow are those most likely to be of interest to the visitor.

Health and Fitness: Great Shape, YMCA, 26 King David Street (tel: 227 111). Inch by Inch, 34 Ben Yehuda Street (17th floor City Tower) (tel: 437 066/436 684). Jerusalem Spa, Hyatt Regency Hotel (tel: 322 906). Samson's Gym, 1 Yoel Salomon Street, Zion Square (tel: 247 526).

Horseback Riding: Amir Ranch Atarot (tel: 852 190). Judean Desert Stables (tel: 241 769). King David Stables, Neve Ilan (tel: 782 898). Kiryat Moshe Riding Club, Beit Hakerem (tel: 533 585).

Swimming: Jerusalem Swimming Pool, 13 'Emeq Refa'im (tel: 632 092). YMCA, 26 King David Street (tel: 227 111). YMHA, 105 Herzog Street (tel: 789 441/780 143/780 442).

Tennis: Israel Tennis Centre, Elmaliach Street, Katamon (tel: 413 866). YMCA, 26 King David Street (tel: 227 111).

DIRECTORY

Arriving	Health Regulations	Public
Camping	Holidays	Transportation
Customs Regulations	Lost Property	Student and Youth
Driving	Media	Travel
Electricity	Money Matters	Telephones
Embassies and	Opening Times	Time
Consulates	Personal Safety	Tipping
Emergency	Pharmacist	Toilets
Telephone	Places of Worship	Tourist Offices
Numbers	Police	Tours and
Entertainment	Post Office	Excursions
Information		Travel Agencies

Arriving

A passport, valid for at least six months after the visit is required for entry into Israel. Citizens of the United States, Canada, Australia, New Zealand and the Irish Republic (Eire) require a visitor's visa, which is issued free at the point of entry, except for nationals of Eire, who must pay the requisite fee. Citizens of the United Kingdom do not require an entry visa. For all visitors it is essential to have a ticket which lists the next destination after Israel. Officials at Israel's ports of entry have been known to turn back travellers who had only a one-way ticket and/or insufficient funds with which to maintain themselves during their stay. It is, therefore, advisable to carry an international credit card as well as travellers' cheques. Visitors may stay for up to three months. An extension of stay can be obtained at the nearest district office of the Ministry of the Interior.

By Air

Jerusalem has an inland airport at Atarot, which is used mainly for domestic flights to and from Eilat, the southern resort city. There are both scheduled and charter flights from Europe to Eilat. Visitors who may want to continue from Eilat to Jerusalem have the options of flying with Arkia to Jerusalem or via Jerusalem to Tel Aviv or Haifa, renting a car, or travelling by bus. Flight time is just under one hour. The journey by car or bus takes six to eight hours. Don't take a taxi from Eilat, as the cost would be exorbitant.

The main international airport is Ben Gurion, located at Lod, 12 miles (20km) from Tel Aviv, and a 30 to 40 minute drive from Jerusalem (about an hour by bus). Israel's national airline, El Al, operates scheduled flights direct to Ben Gurion from New York, London and several European cities. In addition, TWA is the main American carrier on the Israel route, and British Airways has regular scheduled flights from London to Ben Gurion. Flying time from New York to Tel Aviv is nine to eleven hours, and from London around four and a half. Passengers arriving on group tours will be transported by bus from the airport to their hotels. There is also an El Al bus which leaves every hour on the hour between 6:00 A.M. and 10:00 P.M.; and less comfortable Egged buses, which leave at 20 minute intervals between 7:15 A.M. and 6:00 P.M.; the return journey leaves between 6:15 A.M. and 7:00 P.M.

There are rental car agencies (Ansa, Avis, Budget, Eldan, Europcar and Hertz) at the airport, and taxi and *sherut* services outside the arrivals lounge. A *sherut* is a multiple taxi service which takes a maximum of seven passengers depending on the size of the vehicle (for the journey to the airport, book ahead: Nesher Sherut, 21 King George Street, (tel: 227 227.) It is much cheaper than a regular taxi, though a private cab is a better deal for a family of four or

more. Private cabs also impose a small additional charge for luggage. The Ministry of Tourism maintains an information desk in the arrivals lounge where correct rates for taxis can be obtained in advance (as well as information about hotel reservations). Ascertain with the driver what his price is before you get into the cab. If his quote is in excess of the official rate you are at liberty to refuse him and to take the next cab.

When travelling intracity, you *must* insist that the cab driver turn on his meter. If he refuses you may jot down his name and number which, by law, must be prominently displayed within the cab. You can then report him to the Ministry of Tourism, 24 King

There's no shortage of taxis – but you must be sure the driver turns on the meter before setting off

George Street, Jerusalem (tel: 237 311) and/or the Ministry of Transport, Clal Building, 97 Jaffa Road (tel: 229 411).

When leaving from Ben Gurion airport, check in at least two hours before departure; one hour before if you are flying El Al and have checked in your luggage to their office in Jerusalem the evening before departure (except on Fridays, holy days and the eve of holy days). In the second instance, your luggage will be transported to your plane for you.

Keep some cash spare, as all departing passengers must pay an airport tax, which may not have been included in your airfare.

By Sea

The major sea ports of entry to Israel are Haifa and Ashdod. There are regular car ferry services from Piraeus (Greece) to Haifa operated by Stability Line and Afroessa Lines; and from Cyprus (via Egypt) to Haifa, by Louis Guise Lines.

By Road

There is overland access to Israel from Egypt and Jordan but it is more trouble than it's worth. Passengers travel by Egyptian or Jordanian buses to the Israeli border, where they alight and endure a lengthy process of passport and customs control at both exit and entry points. They then transfer to Israeli buses. Arrangements with travel agents should be made well in advance. Buses travel daily between Cairo and Jerusalem. Travel to Jordan is a little more difficult, since Israel and Jordan are technically enemies.

Camping

For details of sites in the vicinity of Jerusalem, see **Accommodation**, page 92. For full details of these and other sites contact the **Israel Camping Union**, POB 53, Nahariyya 22100, Israel. A camping leaflet is available from Israel Government Tourist Offices abroad.

Crime *see* **Personal Safety**

Customs Regulations

For adult tourists entering Israel, the duty-free allowances (for private consumption) include 250 cigarettes or 250g of tobacco or tobacco products; 1 litre of spirits; 2 litres of wine; 0.25 litres of perfume/toilet water; and gifts up to the value US$125, or equivalent including foodstuffs up to $6^1/_2$ lbs (3 kilos) in weight, providing no single food type exceeds 1 kilo.

Visitors may also bring personal photographic and communications equipment into the country, as well as a bicycle, sports and camping equipment, musical instruments and jewellery. These items must be declared on entry. The visitor may be asked to leave a deposit equivalent to the import tax on these goods. This sum is refunded when you leave the country with your goods intact. For the import of flowers, plants and seeds a certificate is required.

There are no restrictions on the import of local or foreign currencies, but when leaving the country you may take out no more than 500 shekel and up to the amount imported in foreign currency.

Driving

Traffic in Israel drives on the right hand side of the road and priority is given to the driver coming from the right—unless otherwise indicated by signs. Road signs are international and are in both English and Hebrew and occasionally in Arabic as well: distances are in kilometres.

Road signs are in English, Hebrew and, sometimes, Arabic too

The speed limit is 31mph (50kph) in built-up areas and 50mph (80kph) on open roads. A word of warning about Israeli drivers: they can drive aggressively and without caution.

Down-town parking in Jerusalem and other urban centres is an endless source of frustration. A red strip on the curb indicates that parking is forbidden. A blue strip permits parking for a fee for a maximum of two hours.

Parking coupons are available from kiosks all over the city. Note that offenders who leave their vehicles even momentarily in a no-parking zone may return to discover that the car has either been towed away or that its mobility has been impeded by a 'Denver boot' (clamp). If your car has been towed away, telephone the police on 100, and you will be told where you can pick it up and pay the fine for your infringement. In the case of a Denver boot, a note will be left on the windshield to notify you where to go to pay the fine to have the boot removed. The fine must be paid in cash in shekels. Within the city proper it is usually easier and faster to take the bus.

Car Breakdown

MEMSI is the Automobile and Touring Club of Israel. Its offices are at 19 Petach Tikva Road, Tel Aviv (tel: (03) 622 961); Clal House, 97 Jaffa Road (Shop 97), Jerusalem (tel: 241 786); 7 Shmaryahu Levin Street, Haifa (tel: (04) 667 824) and Shop 31, Egged Central Bus Station, Beersheba (tel: (057) 70695). MEMSI offers around-the-clock emergency help to members of national Automobile Clubs affiliated with the international organisations AIT or FIA.

Car Rental

Al Ansa International, 19 King David Street, Jerusalem (tel: 222 151).

Ar Car, 8 Pines Street Jerusalem (tel: 385 515 and 384 889); or 8 King David Street, Jerusalem (tel: 240 016).

A Travel Car Ltd, 210 Jaffa Road, Jerusalem (tel: 280 151 and 280

668); or 68 Jaffa Road, Jerusalem (tel: 223 778).

Auto Rentals Ltd, 20 Shlomzion Hamalka Street, Jerusalem (tel: 432 115).

Avis Dan Rent-a-Car Ltd, 22 King David Street, Jerusalem (tel: 249 001).

Budget Rent-a-Car, 14 King David Street, Jerusalem (tel: 248 991).

Eldan Rent-a-Car, Hilton Hotel Building, Jerusalem (tel: 533 030).

Europcar, 8 King David Street, Jerusalem (tel: 248 464).

Geula Rent-a-Car, 20 Itzhak Shollel Street, Jerusalem (tel: 384 914).

Hertz-Kesher Rent-a-Car, 18 King David Street, Jerusalem (tel: 231 351).

Netz Harel Rent-a-Car Ltd, 9 Pines Street, Jerusalem (tel: 384 261 and 382 044).

Orly Rent-a-Car Ltd, 2 Hillel Street, Jerusalem (tel: 240 213).

Shako Land Rent-a-Car, 18 King David Street, Jerusalem (tel: 231 779 and 224 341).

Splendid Car Rental Ltd, 10 King David Street, Jerusalem (tel: 242 553).

Zohar Renta-a-Car, 178 Jaffa Road, Jerusalem (tel: 539 227).

Nearly all car rental services operate on a 24-hour basis. Fleets include mini buses, vans, station wagons, jeeps and air-conditioned limousines with radios and other extras. Most rental agencies are located in King David Street, which is a fairly short street. Local firms are more difficult to find, but tend to be cheaper.

All agencies offer both long- and short-term rentals, and most provide airport delivery and pick-up services. Some also have branches at Ben Gurion airport, and some have desks at the larger hotels.

The minimum age for renting a car varies from 21 to 23, depending on the company. Non-Israelis are required to hold a valid International Driver's Licence, but not all companies insist on this and some will accept US state driver's licences or others that are printed in English or French.

Electricity

Standard voltage in Israel is 220 volts AC. Most plugs are three-pronged but in some places they are also two-pronged. US appliances will need an adaptor, plus, for appliances normally requiring 110/120 volts and without dual-voltage, a voltage transformer (not necessary for appliances normally working off 240 volts).

Embassies and Consulates

Of the numerous countries which have diplomatic relations with Israel, very few have to date been willing to establish embassies in Jerusalem until the political future of the city is resolved. Some countries which do not have embassies in Jerusalem maintain two consulates—one in East and one in West Jerusalem.

As a rule, diplomatic missions are closed on Saturdays and Sundays, but in case of emergency, there is a recorded message with a telephone number where an embassy or consular official can be contacted.

Diplomatic missions in Jerusalem include:

United States: 18 Agron Street
(tel: 234 271), Derekh Shekhem
(tel: 282 231)
United Kingdom: Sheikh Jarrah,
East Jerusalem (tel: 828 281),
Tower House, haRakkevet
Street, near Railway, West
Jerusalem (tel: 717 724)
Australian and Canadian visitors
should approach their
respective embassies in Tel
Aviv:
Australia: 185 Rehov Hayarkon
(tel: (03) 243152)
Canada: 220 Rehov Hayarkon
(tel: (03) 228122)

Emergency Telephone Numbers

The main emergency services
can be contacted on the
following numbers:

Police	100
Fire	102
Medical assistance (ambulance)	101

See also **Health Regulations** for
further emergency numbers.

*Folk dancing is very popular in
Israel, and finding out where to
watch it is no problem*

Entertainment Information

Your best source of information
is *The Jerusalem Post*,
particularly Friday's edition, with
its special pullout, 'In Jerusalem',
which contains listings of all
major events, including film,
theatre, concerts, radio and
television. The Israel
Government Tourist Office
provides copies of *Events in
Jerusalem*.
Recorded information on events
in the Jerusalem area can be
obtained by dialling 244197 after
6:00 P.M., Sunday to Thursday,
and after 2:00 P.M. hrs on Fridays.

Entry Formalities *see* Arriving

Health Regulations

Vaccinations are not required.
Tap water is safe to drink,
though there is a growing trend

towards drinking mineral water, available in large and small bottles in all supermarkets and most soft drink kiosks.

Israel has excellent medical facilities, and tourists may go to all emergency departments and first-aid centres (see also **Pharmacist**). Health centres are marked by the red Star of David on a white background, the sign of Magen David Adom, Israel's equivalent to the Red Cross. For an ambulance, or any medical emergency, just dial 101.

Medical insurance is recommended.

Hospitals and pharmacies which are on duty in the evening during the Jewish Sabbath are listed each Friday in *The Jerusalem Post*, the only English language daily published in Israel.

Hospitals include:

Bikur Holim, 5 Strauss Street (tel: 701 111);

Hadassah Hospital 'En Kerem wing (tel: 427 427; Mt Scopus wing (tel: 818 111);

Shaarei Zedek, Bayit Vegan (tel: 555 111).

Pharmacists:

Super-Pharm, 5 Burla Street (tel: 639 321 and Centre-Pharm, 20 Yad Harutzim Street (tel: 731 475) are open on Saturday nights throughout the year.

Mobile Intensive Care Services: tel: 523 133.

Dental emergency services for hotel guests and other tourists can be reached at 8 Strauss Street (tel: 383 904); and Hadassah 'En Kerem Emergency Dental Clinic (open 10:00 A.M.– 4:00 P.M. on Fridays, Saturdays and Jewish holidays).

Emergency treatment is available on weekends and on holy days through the Magen David Adom (tel: 523133/4 in Jerusalem).

Accident victims who may find themselves in sudden need of a wheelchair or other medical equipment may borrow such items free of charge from the Yad Sarah Organisation, 49 Rehov HaNevi'im, (tel: 244 242).

Holidays

Jewish commercial activity comes to a general halt on Friday afternoons as the nation prepares for the Sabbath. Jews live according to a lunar calendar, and the Jewish leap year, in contrast to the Gregorian leap year, which has an extra day, has a whole extra month. This accounts for the discrepancies in Gregorian calendar dates of Jewish festivals. The Muslims also take their guidelines from a lunar calendar, but whereas the Jewish Sabbath falls on a Saturday, the Muslim Sabbath falls on a Friday. Many Muslim merchants prefer to keep their establishments closed on Fridays.

The most important periods in the Muslim calendar are Id el Adha, a four-day sacrificial festival (December/January); New Year (January/February); Mohammed's Birthday (April); Ramadan (October), the holiest month in the calendar, commemorating the revelation of the Koran to Mohammed; and Id el Fitr (October/November), three days of feasting which mark the end of Ramadan. Observed in the ninth month of the Muslim calendar, Ramadan is a period of austerity in which food, drink and other pleasures are banned from dawn to dusk. The Christian holidays of both the Latin and the Eastern Churches are observed by the various Christian communities, but the only Christian holidays of which the population at large has any awareness are Easter and Christmas.

Jewish Holidays have the greatest significance. The main Jewish festivals are as follows (for detailed descriptions of the Festivities see **Special Events**, page 100):

Rosh Hashana: (September or October)

Yom Kippur (September/ October)

Succot (September/October)

Simchat Torah (September/ October)

Hanukka (November/ December)

Tu B'Shvat (January/February)

Purim (February/March)

Pesach (March/April)

Shavuot (May/June)

Tisha B'Av (July/August)

Other important calendar dates in Israel are:

Independence Day, which falls in April or May and celebrates the renewed nationhood of an ancient people;

Lag B'Omer, also in April or May, the 33rd day after Pesach, marked by weddings and bonfires; and **Jerusalem Liberation Day**, in May or June, to celebrate the anniversary of the reunification of the city. There are also two days of mourning during this period, **Remembrance Day for Fallen Soldiers**, and **Martyrs' Remembrance Day**. On the

mornings of both days, the nation comes to a halt for two minutes at the blowing of a siren and restaurants and cinemas are closed in the evening.

Lost Property

Losses and thefts should be reported as quickly as possible to the police at the Russian Compound in Jaffa Road in West Jerusalem or the Kishle, inside the Jaffa Gate in East Jerusalem. The emergency telephone number for police is 100.

Media

Newspapers* Bearing in mind Israel's unique geopolitical situation, news is important to the Israelis, a fact reflected in the existence of over two dozen daily newspapers. *The Jerusalem Post* is the English language daily, though it is not published on Saturday (see also **Entertainment Information**). There is a monthly magazine, *In English*, which deals with current affairs. Other English language periodicals dealing with military matters and the history and geography of the country are on sale at Steimatzky stores in downtown Jerusalem, as well as in hotel book stores. Major American, British and Canadian publications are available at these stores. At hotels and news-stands you will also find most papers from home, a day or so late.

Radio *Kol Israel* (Voice of Israel) operates five stations and offers a mixture of pop, rock and talk, plus news three times a day. Its English language broadcasts are on 576 Khz and 1458 Khz at 7:00 A.M., 1:00 , 5:00 and 8:00 P.M.

Where history is still in the making news is important. There are numerous papers on sale daily

The Voice of Peace, which broadcasts mostly in English, can be picked up between 6:00 A.M. and 3:00 A.M. Voice of America and BBC broadcasts come across loud and clear from 5:09 A.M.

Television* Stations broadcast in Hebrew and Arabic, though many entertainment programmes and movies are imports from the United States or Britain, which may be subtitled rather than dubbed. Jordan Television offers competing entertainment. Daily newspapers carry details of programmes.

* At the time of going to press, plans are underway for the presentation of a nightly television news service in English; and in the print media, arrangements are being finalised for a new, sleek English language weekly.

DIRECTORY

Money Matters

The Israeli unit of currency is the shekel (NIS) which comes in banknote denominations of NIS100, NIS50, NIS20, NIS10 and NIS5. Coins are divided into denominations of NIS5, NIS1, NIS$^{1}/_{2}$, 10 agorot, 5 agorot and 1 agora. There are 100 agorot in a shekel. The shekels are referred to as new shekels, although it was in 1985 that old shekels disappeared from the market. The new shekels were introduced as a measure to curb inflation.

Travellers' cheques and hard currencies, especially US dollars, are accepted as payment in lieu of local currency, but visitors could find themselves short-changed, not only because they get a lower rate of exchange than in the bank, but also because cab drivers and food store personnel will not calculate the VAT exemption due to customers who make their payments in foreign currencies.

Banks open at 8:.30 A.M. on Sunday to Friday. Some close at 12:30 P.M. and reopen for one to three hours at 4:00 P.M. Others are open all day. Some are closed on Monday afternoons. All banks are closed on Friday afternoons. Branches in the leading hotels offer additional banking hours.

Major international credit cards are widely accepted.

Opening Times

Shops Supermarkets and grocery stores are open from 7:00 A.M. Some supermarkets are open around the clock from 7:00 A.M. Wednesday till 2:00 P.M. Friday, and reopen again soon after sunset on Saturdays.

Shops and offices are closed on Saturdays in West Jerusalem but are open in East Jerusalem, depending on the political climate.

Shops in Jerusalem usually stay open till 7:00 P.M.; some close a little later. Some supermarkets stay open till midnight. Downtown stores open between 8:30 and 9:30 A.M. Some stay open all day. Others close between 1:00 and 4:00 P.M. Some are closed on Tuesday afternoons.

Offices mostly open at 8:30 A.M. **Restaurants** and **coffee shops** vary in their opening times. Some are open at 7:00 A.M. There are at least two coffee shops—Le Croissant, in the cinema district, and Home Plus, near the Russian Compound—which open around the clock.

Museums see **What To See** for individual times

Banks see **Money Matters**

Personal Safety

Although the international media have magnified political unrest in Jerusalem out of all proportion, there are plenty of visitors to the city who prefer to believe the evidence of their own eyes. It is true that people have been injured and even killed by gasoline bombs, well-aimed stones and knife-wielding nationalists; but on the whole, Jerusalem has a much better record for personal security than New York, London or Paris. People are generally safe, but their possessions, unfortunately, are not. Jerusalem may be the Holy City but that does not make Israel's capital immune to

Tension sometimes runs high in Jerusalem, but people are normally perfectly safe

thieves, con artists and cheats. There are quite a few pickpockets, but street thieves usually go for the throat to grab all that glitters. Too much gold chain just invites trouble. Similarly, be careful about wearing shoulder bags. Thieves will often cut the straps and run off with your passport, your credit cards, your plane tickets, your money and anything else you may have been carrying. Keep your bags tightly under your arms or wear a money belt. If you are swarthy in appearance, you may be stopped by police or military personnel and asked to produce proof of your identity. Make sure that you carry your passport with you at all times.

Pharmacist

There is no dearth of pharmacies in either East or West Jerusalem. They all, however, deal only with Western medicines. Visitors staying in East Jerusalem will find pharmacies in Salah-ed-Din Street. These are open on Saturdays. West Jerusalem visitors will find pharmacies in the Talpiot Industrial Zone shopping centre, Nayot, Gaza Road, on the corner of Hillel and King George Streets, in King George Street near the Hamashbir department store, in the Ben Yehuda Mall, in Jaffa Road near Zion Square, in Jaffa Road opposite the Ben Yehuda Market, in Jaffa Road on either side of the Central Bus Terminal and in the main shopping centres of all suburbs.

For visitors staying at the Hyatt Hotel, which is technically in East Jerusalem, there are pharmacies in the nearby French Hill and Ramot Eshkol shopping centres. The Mount Scopus wing of Hadassah Hospital is only five minutes' walk from the hotel. *The Jerusalem Post* and its 'In Jerusalem' weekend supplement each list the names, addresses and phone numbers of emergency pharmacies and hospitals.

Arabs have many herbal remedies for a wide range of ailments. As a rule, these are not available in pharmacies, but they are certainly well known in the village communities. The visitor who strikes up a conversation with English-speaking Arabs in the Old City will sooner or later come across someone who can recommend an expert in the art of healing.

DIRECTORY

Places of Worship

Of the close to half a million residents in Jerusalem, some 80 per cent are of the Jewish faith. Muslims account for around 17 per cent of the capital's population, and the rest are Christians. Although the Christians are relatively small in number, the diverse Christian denominations are well represented. Some are listed below.

Notre Dame, built as a hostel for Catholic pilgrims

Anglican

Christ Church, Jaffa Gate (tel: 282 082)
St George's Cathedral, 20 Nablus Road (tel: 283 302)

Baptist

Baptist Centre, 35 Nablus Road (tel: 283 258)

First Baptist Bible Church, Salah-ed-Din Street (tel: 282 118)
Southern Baptist Convention, 4 Narkiss Street (tel: 225 942)

Catholic

Armenian, 41 Via Dolorosa (tel: 284 262)
Coptic, St Francis Street (tel: 282 868)
Maronite, 25 Maronite Road (tel: 282 158)
Notre Dame, Paratroopers Road (Rehov Hatzanchanim) opposite New Gate (tel: 289 723)
St Saviours, 1 St Francis Street (tel: 282 868)
St Stephens, Nablus Road (tel: 282 213)

Christian Science

East Jerusalem YMCA, 29 Nablus Road (tel: 282 375)

Interdenominational

Garden Tomb, Nablus Road (tel: 283 402)

Lutheran

Church of the Redeemer, Muristan Road (tel: 282 543)
Danish, 12 Gihon Street (tel: 724 188)
Finnish, 25 Shivte Yisra'el Street (tel: 288 631)
Norwegian, 26 Hatzfira Street (tel: 638 923)
Swedish, 58 Prophets Street (tel: 223 822)

Mormon

Brigham Young Centre, between Mount of Olives and Mount Scopus (tel: 273 181)

Orthodox

Armenian, Armenian Patriarchate Road (tel: 282 331)
Coptic, Via Dolorosa (tel: 282 343)
Ethiopian, Eighth Station of the Cross (tel: 282 848)

Greek Orthodox, Greek Patriarchate Road (tel: 284 917)
Roumanian, 46 Shivte Yisra'el Street (tel: 287 355)
Russian Ecclesiastical Mission St Mary Magdalene, Gethsemane (tel: 282 897)
Russian Orthodox Mission, Russian Compound, Jaffa Road (tel: 222 565)
Syrian, St Mark's Road (tel: 283 304)

Presbyterian
St Andrews Church of Scotland, Rakevet Street (tel: 717 701)

Seventh Day Adventists
4 Abraham Lincoln Street (tel: 221 547)
Il Ibn Telev Street (tel: 283 271)
The overwhelming majority of churches are located inside the Old City walls, and the easiest access, in most cases, is via the New Gate. Visitors to the Armenian Church will find it more convenient to enter via the Jaffa or Zion Gates.

Mosques
The most important and impressive mosques in Jerusalem are located on and around the Temple Mount, inside the walls of the Old City. They include:
Dome of the Chain
Dome of the Rock
El-Aqsa
Mosque of Omar
White Mosque

Jewish
Central Synagogue Bet haKerem, 17 Bet haKerem Road (tel: 537 643)
Centre for Conservative Judaism, 4 Agron Street (tel: 223 539)
Chabad Synagogues: Jewish Quarter Old City and 16 Yermiyahu Street, Romema (tel: 814 755)
Great Synagogue (orthodox) 56 King George Street (tel: 247 112)
Israel Goldstein Synagogue, Hebrew University, Giv'at Ram (tel: 585 886)
Italian Synagogue, 27 Hillel Street (tel: 241 610)
The Union for Progressive Judaism, 13 King David Street (tel: 232 444)
Toldot Aharon (ultra orthodox), 35 Shivte Yisra'el Street (tel: 322 545)
Yeshurun, King George Street, corner of Shemu'el haNaggid (tel: 243 942)

Jewish services are also held daily at the Western Wall.

Further details of places of worship may be obtained from **The Ministry for Religious Affairs**, 236 Jaffa Road, near the Central Bus Terminal (tel: 532 118); the **Office of the Chief Rabbinate**, 58 King George Street, (tel: 249 811); or from the **Christian Information Centre**, Jaffa Gate (tel: 287 647).

Police
Most police understand some English. Many speak English quite fluently. But in case you are mugged or robbed in the street, and come across a policeman who doesn't know any English, use this sentence in Hebrew: *Na tavi li mishehu shemedaber Anglit.* This means: 'Please bring me someone who speaks English.' If you are too agitated to remember the sentence, just keep on repeating the word *Anglit.* He will get the message. The police emergency number

in all parts of the country is 100. If the number is engaged for too long a period, callers from Jerusalem should try 391 111. Tourism police, who speak foreign languages, can be contacted at 273 222.

Post Office

Look out for a white stag on a blue background, the symbol of the Israeli Post Office. The Central Post Office at 23 Jaffa Road, across the road from the Mayoral Office, is only a few minutes' walk from the Jaffa Gate. Its facsimile, telex and telegram services are open around the clock, except on Fridays, when it closes for the Sabbath two to three hours before sunset. Other postal services at the Central Post Office are in operation between 8:00 A.M. and 7:00 P.M. Stamps are available in hotels and at all kiosks and newsagents displaying a white stag sticker or metal plaque.

There are local post offices in most suburbs, but they close earlier than the Central Post Office, and not all of them offer fax services to the general public. Visitors staying in the hotel belt in and around King George Street can make use of the post office in Keren Hayesod Street. Those staying in East Jerusalem can go to the post office in Salah-ed-Din Street. This particular post office is open throughout the morning on Saturdays.

Mail boxes are red and carry the white stag logo. Mail to US destinations takes around two weeks to arrive.

Telegrams can be sent by phone and charged to the number of the telephone subscriber. To send a telephone cable call 171. The switchboard number at the Central Post Office is 230 672.

Public Transportation

Buses

Israel's public transportation system is reasonably inexpensive. Jerusalemites who don't have their own cars get around by bus, taxi or *sherut* (seven-seater shared taxi). A few brave souls ride bicycles or motorcycles; and the younger generation use skateboards if they don't have to travel too far. Although the bus services are excellent, the city's population explosion has taken its toll on bus transportation efficiency. Many of the down-town streets are too narrow for a two-way flow of motorised traffic, with the result that at certain times of the day the congestion seems endless.

The buses are frequently crowded, and bus rides are made uncomfortable by soldiers' large, sausage-shaped kit-bags which block the aisles, together with babies' strollers, hikers' back-packs and the loaded shopping bags of passengers going home from markets.

The bus system is confusing for the visitor because the destination of the bus is not displayed—only the number. Bus schedules can be obtained from the information booth at the Egged Central Bus Terminal, but they are not always available in English. *Your Jerusalem*, a monthly publication available free of charge at supermarkets and hotel reception desks, has both a bus-line map and an

Buses show route numbers, not destinations: you need a bus map

alphabetical short list of destinations and buses which travel to or near those places. There is no need to give the driver the exact fare; but at the same time there is no guarantee that he or she will have change. If you intend to be in Jerusalem for three or four days, it is cheaper and more convenient to purchase a bus ticket which gives the holder the right to 25 bus rides. The ticket can be bought on the bus, and the driver punches a hole in it each time it is used. The ticket can be used by more than one person at a time. Minibuses operate in Tel Aviv, but not in Jerusalem. One of the musts in Jerusalem is an orientation ride around the city on **Route 99**, the **Jerusalem Circular Line**. The tour, with 34 stops, covers an extraordinarily broad canvas of the city – it travels to points near the Old City, most West Jerusalem sites,

Mount of Olives and Mount Scopus, with pick-up points close to the major hotel areas and is one of the best bargains you can get. There are three ticket options: a single tour ticket, which becomes invalid as soon as you get off the bus; a one-day ticket, which allows you to get off at any stop along the route and to continue the journey on the next bus without any extra charge; and, for people with more time at their disposal, a two-day ticket, giving unlimited travel along the route. The essential benefit of both the second and the third options is that passengers who are interested in specific areas along the route can alight to get their bearings and to take note of the regular bus routes to use if they want to come back under their own steam. The Circular Line operates from 9:00 A.M. to 5:00 P.M. Sunday to Thursday, and on Fridays and the eve of Jewish holy days, when the last stop is at 2:00 P.M.

DIRECTORY

Travellers are supplied with a map of the route, and can listen to a live or recorded explanation while driving from place to place. Departure is from the Egged Bus Terminal near the Jaffa Gate every hour, on the hour. Passengers who want to see Yad Vashem (the Holocaust Museum), should make sure that they take a morning or early afternoon ride, as the last journey of the day does not include Yad Vashem. The telephone number at the Jaffa Gate Terminal is 247 783 or 248 144. Even though there may be a 99 Bus Stop outside your hotel, don't rely on the word of the front desk clerk that the bus will come in 15 minutes. Check the information at one of the above telephone numbers.

Sherut

A *Sherut* is a multiple, shared taxi service, taking up to seven passengers, and is much cheaper than a regular taxi.

Taxis

These can be flagged down in the street or hailed at cab stands in various parts of the city. Usually, the easiest way to get a taxi when you're in a hurry is to get to the nearest hotel and ask the concierge or the front desk to call a cab for you. Drivers generally know enough English to understand where you want to go. If not, one of their dispatchers will. If a driver who speaks only Hebrew or Arabic has radio contact with his dispatcher, point to the radio hook-up on the dashboard and say *Anglit*, which is Hebrew for English. You can make sure of not being overcharged by insisting that the driver turn on

the meter. Some drivers will want to bargain the fare; if so, make sure you agree on a price before you set off. If the driver is unfamiliar with the address, and you don't have a map with you to show him where you're going, take another cab.

All-night taxis include **Rehavia** (tel: 224444) and **Palmach** (tel: 666662 and 666617).

Occasionally, a cab driver will pull up alongside a bus stop and offer to take people along the same route as the bus for half a shekel more than the bus fare. Smoking in buses and taxis is forbidden in Israel. Cab drivers often violate the law, but if you are a non-smoker you are within your rights to request the driver to get rid of his cigarette.

Trains

Israel's train system is far from extensive and trains tend to be old and slow-moving, though cheaper than buses and operating on some picturesque routes. Jerusalem to Tel Aviv is particularly attractive, winding through the Judean Hills. Trains also connect Jerusalem with Haifa, Beersheba, Dimona, and Nahariya. Few locals use trains because they are both irregular and unbearably slow compared to bus and *sherut* options, but for tourists with time to spare the train represents a good value for local or inter-city travel.

Travel on Sabbaths and Other Jewish Holy Days

The regular Egged Bus service does not operate on Friday nights nor during the daylight hours of Saturday or other Jewish holy days. The Arab bus services in East Jerusalem do operate, but they travel primarily to Arab towns and villages, and not to West Jerusalem. Taxis and *sheruts* operate in both East and West Jerusalem, and the fare is slightly higher than it is the rest of the week. There is no train service out of Jerusalem on Saturdays.

Student and Youth Travel
Students in possession of an International Student Identity Card qualify for a 10 per cent discount on Egged inter-city bus services and a 25 per cent reduction on Israel Railways. Other discounts may apply: for example, museum admission prices. Make a point of always carrying your card.
The Israel Student Travel Association (ISTA) offers low-priced tours and programmes of interest to student travellers. They can be contacted in Jerusalem at 5 Elissar Street (tel: 225 288); or Tel Aviv at 109 Ben Yehuda Street (tel: 247 164).

Telephones
Public phones are operated by telephone tokens, available from post offices, kiosks, news agents

As well as booths, there are public telephones in shops and cafés

DIRECTORY

and hotel reception desks. It requires one token to make a local call and several to make inter-city calls. As well as streetside booths, telephones in pharmacies, shops and restaurants are often available for public use, for local calls only.

International calls can be made from some public phones, and signs to this effect are prominently displayed over the phone booths.

It is much cheaper to use a public phone than to call from one's room in the hotel. Collect calls can be made from all public phones. Notwithstanding the increased efficiency of Bezek, the company responsible for Israel's telephone communications, public phones are often out of order. To make sure that you don't lose your telephone token, check the window on the phone to see whether other tokens are visible. If they are, it is a sign that the phone is out of order. If the phone is in proper working order, but the number you have called does not answer, the token can be retrieved by raising the metal protrusion on the bottom right-hand side of the phone. The Hebrew word for token is *asimon*. The plural is *asimonim*.

All regions within the country have area codes. When dialing a Jerusalem or environs number, there is no need to add the 02 area code for Jerusalem. The code for Tel Aviv is 03, Haifa 04 and 059 for Eilat.

As in all parts of the world, directories quickly disappear from phone booths, aside from which, the Israeli directories are mainly in Hebrew. If you are searching for a number and you have the full name and address of the person you want to call, you can obtain it by dialling 144. Most operators speak English.

It is possible to dial direct to most countries of the world from Israel. Instructions enabling you to make these calls will be found alongside phones where this is possible.

To call via the international exchange dial 188. To phone Jerusalem from abroad dial the international access code 010, followed by the Israel country code, 972, then 2 (the city code minus the initial '0') and lastly, the subscriber's number.

Time

For most of the year Jerusalem is seven hours ahead of New York, Washington, Boston, Montreal and Quebec; eight hours ahead of Chicago; 10 hours ahead of Los Angeles; two hours ahead of London and Dublin; nine hours behind Canberra, Melbourne and Sydney, and six hours behind Perth. The recently introduced Summer Time means that clocks in Jerusalem are advanced one hour in spring and turned back one hour in the autumn.

Tipping

A 15 per cent service charge is added at hotel and 'better' restaurants. Where no service charge is made, tipping in restaurants and bars of around 10–15 per cent of the bill is customary.

Hotel porters and chambermaids also expect a

little extra. Taxi drivers do not anticipate a tip from local clientele, but some may be brash enough to ask a tourist for a tip. Those who find an excuse not to turn on their meters should not be tipped, as they have already calculated their tip into the price. Whatever they earn when the meter is off is not shared with the taxation authorities.

Toilets

Public toilets are few and far between, and not always as clean as they should be. Public toilets can be found in Harav Kook Street, near Zion Square, in the small park adjacent to the Ministry of Tourism in King George Street; in Independence Park near the Agron Street entrance; and in the Liberty Bell Gardens. Most restaurants and all cinemas have toilet facilities. The Hamashbir store has toilets located on its upper floors. The best bet is to use hotel toilets.

Unofficial guides abound: look for official information at this sign

Tourist Offices

Jerusalem is first and foremost a pilgrim city, attracting the faithful from all over the world. The **Ministry of Tourism** maintains offices abroad to provide information about Jerusalem and the rest of Israel. It also maintains a 24-hour service at Ben Gurion Airport, as well as information offices, which are open at regular office hours, at 24 King George Street in West Jerusalem (tel: 241 281 and 241 282) and just inside the Jaffa Gate in East Jerusalem (tel: 282 295 and 282 296). These offices are open Sunday to Thursday 8:30A.M. to 5:00P.M., and Friday until 1:00P.M. Just a little further down inside the Jaffa Gate is the **Christian Information Centre** (tel: 287 647). Tourists may also get information through the **Voluntary Tourist Service**, which maintains desks in most 5-star hotels.

There are six Israel Government Tourist Offices (IGTO) in the United States. Chicago: 5 South Wabash Avenue (tel: 312 - 782 4306/7/8). Los Angeles: 6380 Wilshire Boulevard (tel: 213 - 658 7462/3). Miami: Suite 326, 420 Lincoln Road, Miami Beach (tel: 305-673-6862). New York: 350 Fifth Avenue, 19th Floor (tel: 212 - 560-0650). San Francisco: Suite 550, 220 Montgomery Street (tel: 415-775-5462/3/4). Washington: 3514 International Drive, NW (tel: 202-364-5500).

The Canadian IGTO premises are located at Suite 700, 180 Bloor Street West, Toronto, Ontario (tel: 416-964-3784). The IGTO office serving the United Kingdom, is at 18 Great Marlborough Street, London W1V 1AF (tel: 071 434 3651). There is no representative of the

DIRECTORY

IGTO in Australia or New Zealand; the office in San Francisco should be contacted.

Tours and Excursions

Walking Tours are very popular in Jerusalem. Some are provided free and others have a range of prices. The cheaper tours are just rambles with superficial explanations by the guide; the more expensive tours are far more in depth. There are plenty of guide books available with step-by-step walking tours and historical background. You can go at your own pace, and if something strikes your fancy along the way, you don't have to beg an impatient guide to permit you to linger for another few minutes. You can easily tour the Old City by yourself, exploring the colourful bazaars, the art galleries and the holy places; and on the following day, you can just as easily trek around West Jerusalem.

Visitors find there are ways and means of getting around the Mount of Olives...

Bus Tours From the point of view of orientation for first-time visitors, the 99 Bus Route is a must. The bus has more than 30 stops throughout the city, but it's best to start at the beginning of the route which is at the Egged terminal opposite the Citadel, not far from the Jaffa Gate. See also **Buses** under **Public Transportation**

Egged Tours conduct half-day to seven-day tours within Jerusalem and to many other parts of the country. Recommended places to visit include Masada (25 miles/40km), the mountaintop fortress where Jewish martyrs, facing encroaching Roman legions, committed suicide, preferring death to slavery; Jericho (22 miles/35km), the oldest traces of settlement dating back to 8,000 BC; the Dead Sea

(28 miles/45km), with nine times more salt than the Mediterranean, and Qumran. Longer tours might include Galilee and the Golan Heights, the Judean Desert, the Negev Desert and Eilat. For Bethlehem, see under **What to See**, page 68. Details are available at **Egged Tours** offices at the Central Bus Station, Jaffa Road (tel: 304 868); the Reservations Centre 220 Jaffa Road (tel: 304 422); Zion Square, 44a Jaffa Road and at the terminal opposite the Jaffa Gate (tel: 248 144).

Egged also offers Israbus passes, allowing unlimited transport on Egged bus lines throughout the country, and valid for seven days; 14 days; 21 days or for 30 days. A pass also qualifies you for a 15 per cent discount at Egged station restaurants. Before rushing to buy these tickets, calculate whether or not you are getting a bargain. If you only intend travelling backwards and forwards between Jerusalem and Tel Aviv each day, then it is cheaper to buy a regular ticket. But if you intend to travel the full length of the country from the north to the south, then the Israbus tickets represent a considerable saving. Egged Tours also sell bus tickets to Cairo. Buses depart daily at 6:45 A.M. from the Central Bus Station. Other bus companies offering tours include **Galilee Tours**, whose reservation office is at Centre 1, the shopping and hotel complex at the entrance to the city (tel: 383 460); and **United Tours**, in the King David Hotel annexe (tel: 222 187).

All three companies offer more or less the same options. Discounts of 20 per cent on daily tours are given to children under the age of 12. They also receive a 10 per cent discount on overnight accommodation. Neither Egged Tours nor United Tours accepts children under the age of five.

Don't be fooled by tourist brochures which may list up to a dozen stops on your half-day bus tour. Most are within easy walking distance of each other. **Chauffered Cars** driven by trained and qualified tour guides can be hired from **Eshkolot Tours**, 36 Keren haYessod Street (tel: 635 555/665555).

Travel Agencies

Most people who come to visit Jerusalem know exactly where they are going next. Other than new immigrants, few people are allowed into the country on a one-way ticket. So visitors don't really have that much need of local travel agencies. But some do change their travel plans. For instance, until they are actually in Israel, few people realise how easy it is to get to Egypt. Visitors who may need a travel agency may contact: **Ambassador Tours**, 25 King George Street (tel: 244 406) **Diesenhaus** 25 Jaffa Road (tel: 245 932) **Melia**, 33 King George Street (tel: 226 381) **Ophir Tours**, King David Hotel (tel: 222 777) **Orient Shipping**, 19a Keren haYessod Street (tel: 223 004) **Promised Land**, 10 Hillel Street (tel: 233 371) **Ziontours**, 23 Hillel Street (tel: 233 326)

LANGUAGE

The official language of Israel is Hebrew, but Arabic continues to be taught as a first language in Arab schools. In Me'a She'arim, where Hebrew is seldom used in day-to-day communication between one person and another, the language of instruction is Yiddish. Hebrew, Arabic and Yiddish are all written from right to left. Street signs all over the country are written in Hebrew, English and Arabic. To be on the safe side, ask the hotel receptionist to write down your destination in Hebrew so that you may show it to the cab driver, the bus driver or the passer-by in the street. Although it is handy to have a few words in Arabic, it is not really necessary, as those Arabs who do business with tourists have picked up enough from numerous other languages to understand you. Still, it never hurts to say thank you in Arabic, which is *shukran*.

A Hebrew Glossary follows:

Basic Vocabulary
can you speak English? *ha'Im ata yachol ledaber Anglit?* (Masculine)
ha'm at yechola ledaber Anglit? (Feminine)
hello or goodbye *shalom*
good morning *boker tov*
good evening *erev tov*
pardon me *slicha*
thank you *todah*
please *bevakasha*
how much does it cost? *kama ze oleh?*
yes *Cain*
no *lo*
how long does it take? *kama zman ze yikach*
bus *autobus*
taxi *monit*
what time is it? *ma hasha'a?*

where are the toilets? *eifo hasherutim?*
money *kessef*
cash *mezuman*
credit card *cartis ashrei*

Food
bread *lechem*
milk *chalav*
cheese *gevina*
jam *riba*
water *mayim*
breakfast *aruchat boker*
lunch *aruchat tzochorayim*
dinner *aruchat erev*
meat *basar*
vegetables *yerakot*
fruit *perot*

Numerals
1 *achat*
2 *shtayim*
3 *shalosh*
4 *arba*
5 *hamesh*
6 *shesh*
7 *sheva*
8 *shmone*
9 *tesha*

10 *eser*
11 *ahad esrei*
12 *shtayim esrei*
20 *esrim*
30 *shloshim*
40 *arbaim*
50 *hamishim*
60 *shishim*
70 *shivim*

80 *shmonim*
90 *tishim*
100 *meah*
1,000 *elef*

INDEX

INDEX/ACKNOWLEDGEMENTS

The Automobile Association would like to thank the following photographers & libraries for their assistance in the preparation of this book:

ANTONY SOUTER took all the photographs (© AA Photo Library) except:

J ALLAN CASH PHOTO LIBRARY 63 Montefiore's windmill.

INTERNATIONAL PHOTOBANK Cover: Dome of the Rock

NATURE PHOTOGRAPHERS LTD 69 Dry wadi (R Tidman), 70 Red sea crownfish (D Smith), 72 Salt crystals (R Tidman), 73 Ibex (M Muller & H Wohlmuth), 74 Desert (R Tidman), 76 Glossy ibis (J Karmadi).

ZEFA PICTURE LIBRARY UK LTD 101 Festival of Purim, 103 Jewish Festival of Lights.

Antony Souter would like to thank STC Travel for their help.